Duck Shooting

By the same author

Sport

Come Fishing with Me
Come Fly-Fishing with Me
Angler's Encyclopaedia
The ABC of Fishing (Editor)
The Gun-Punt Adventure
Kenzie, the Wild Goose Man
The Bedside Wildfowler (Editor)
Town Gun
The ABC of Shooting (Editor)

Humour

Rod, Pole or Perch
Dudley: The Worst Dog in the World

DUCK SHOOTING

Colin Willock

ANDRE DEUTSCH

For Richard Arnold, Aubrey Buxton, Ted Eales, John Gray, Jack Hargreaves, Don Legget, Malcolm Monteith, the late Kenzie Thorpe, John Richardson and many other good fowling companions.

First published 1962
This revised edition first published 1981
by André Deutsch Limited
105 Great Russell Street, London WC1

ISBN 233 97039 8

Photoset in Great Britain by
Rowland Phototypesetting Limited
Bury St Edmunds, Suffolk
and printed by
St Edmundsbury Press
Bury St Edmunds, Suffolk

CONTENTS

LIST OF ILLUSTRATIONS

Plates

Figures in the text

All photographs by Pamela Harrison FRPS

The identification drawings are by R. A. Richardson and are reproduced by courtesy of the Wildfowlers' Association of Great Britain and Ireland from their pamphlet *Know Your Quary*.

DUCK SHOOTING

I shot my first duck on the North Kent salt marshes at the close of a freezing, calm, and otherwise bagless December day. We had slogged out in the dark a mile over what must surely be the muddiest mud in the western hemisphere. We had crouched, frozen, on islands while the tide rose around us and dropped again. Then, in the reddening dusk of late afternoon, we plodded back. During the whole of this time I doubt if we had seen a single duck within three gunshots' range. The day had been too calm and too clear, but I hadn't really cared for it was my first meeting with the saltings, and that had been enough. The smells, the sights, the sounds of the marsh had bitten into me like a strong acid and left a mark that is clearly etched to this day.

When we had climbed out of the last gutter, and as we stood beneath the grass bank of the sea wall, there suddenly came a whisper of wings. No one else can have been paying attention, which was surprising for the other two were experienced fowlers. I heard the sound and looked hard out to sea. There, the sky was clear and frosty and quite hopeless as a background against which to pick up a flying bird. Suddenly a duck flicked out of the opaque part of the evening sky and flew into the glow left by the sun. I don't know how I did it, for I was a very poor shot in those days, but I nailed the duck in that split-second with an old single-barrelled 12-bore, and it fell, stone dead, into the water now running fast out of the creek. I floundered down the mud bank and threw myself on the duck as if I couldn't really believe I had got it. It was a fine big mallard drake.

I've been a duck shooter before everything else, ever since. Pheasants are all very well and I admit that at their best they present a shot that probably outclasses most things a duck can do – if you'll except a teal in a gale of wind. But pheasants, even when they are 'wild' birds, are essentially artificial. They don't belong here. They don't get here under their own steam. They're cunning and artful, and they've adapted themselves magnificently to the British countryside, but that's as far as it goes. They lack the magic that belongs to the wild duck and wild goose. They are not, in fact, wild at all. When you talk about a wild pheasant you use the word in inverted commas; it simply means 'not hand-reared'. Duck are wild as a hawk is wild, and it is significant that the towniest townsman naturally uses the expressions wild duck and wild geese, even though he knows little about either.

Part of the mystique of wild fowl lies, I think, in the distances these birds travel on migration, and in the fact that they come to us from such unimaginably lonely places. Their habit of moving about at great speed at dawn and dusk adds to their mystery, and a wedge of mallard at full pelt against the moon is something that might even stop dead the heart of a ballroom-dancing champion between beats of the quickstep.

I said that there was no such thing as a non-wild duck. This is not quite true, for it is becoming more and more the fashion to rear mallard as you rear pheasants.

Landowners do it. Shooting syndicates do it. Even wildfowling clubs do it. There is certainly no harm in it, and as far as the wildfowlers go it is a worthwhile piece of general conservation. Wildfowlers shoot birds out on the marshes, so they feel they should replace stock. This is an admirable thing, but then wildfowlers are often naturalists. Furthermore, the ringed birds released by wildfowling clubs all help in the study of duck migration. But if the idea is to rear mallard for shooting then I feel certain you are producing a poor second best, for hand-reared mallard show an awful reluctance to leave the home water and will usually fly round and round, getting higher and higher, as more and more guns go off. They certainly bear little resemblance to the real thing and I wouldn't like any gun whose only experience is with home bred duck to run away with the idea that he has been duck shooting. He hasn't. He has simply shot at duck. Still, if the sight of mallard in flight has kindled the smallest spark of admiration, there's hope for him in the future, hope that he will go and hunt – and hunt, the term the Americans use, is the right word in this case – less the genuine article.

This book is an attempt to make clear how the genuine article can be found.

First, a piece of heartening information. At this date (1980) there is no shortage of duck in Britain. This is largely due to the good sense of a number of people of apparently contrary interests, and to a paradoxical piece of good fortune.

To deal with the good fortune first. Though it is

quite true that development schemes have claimed many parts of the coast that were formerly duck haunts, and that inland drainage has tended in the same direction, there is one big way in which the spread of human population has helped the spread of the wildfowl population. As the cities expand, so their citizens need more water. The reservoirs built to supply this water are perfect resting places, and also feeding places, for enormous numbers of duck. The London reservoirs are, perhaps, the most dramatic in this respect, and more are still being built. Stand at dawn on the baffle bank that reaches three quarters of a mile out into the three-mile-wide waters of the Queen Mary reservoir, Staines, and you will see a morning flight that would not disgrace the Beauly Firth or parts of the Solway. Mallard, teal, pintail, shoveler, wigeon in really hard weather, tufted duck in clouds in any weather, pochard, mergansers, goosanders, occasional smews, goldeneye, Canadas and even grey geese can all be seen there on the wing or on the water in vast rafts. There are many more reservoirs as rich as the 'Mary' in wildfowl in and around London and also nearer to the coast. Abberton reservoir in Essex, close to the Blackwater estuary, holds many thousands of wigeon, during the winter. The excellent thing about all these huge stretches of water is that they are rarely disturbed. They therefore make perfect resting grounds during the daytime when duck need a minimum of disturbance. It is not the number of duck shot that is the danger to the species, even though hundreds fall to a single gun in a season. The latter is very much the exception where wildfowling is concerned. Continual blasting both on roosting and feeding grounds does the damage.

This brings me to the second point – the co-operation of apparently opposed interests. Where wildfowl conservation is concerned great common sense has won the day, and the most improbable of marriages has come about. It is, indeed, a shotgun wedding, for the parties are the Nature Conservancy, the Royal Society for the Protection of Birds and the Wildfowl Trust on one side, and the sportsmen represented by the Wildfowlers' Association of Great Britain and Ireland* on the other.

While the anti-blood sports battle rages fiercely and emotionally, and illogically, in practically every other field from fishing to stag-hunting, the duck shooters and the duck watchers and conservers have rightly seen that they have the same object in view – namely to maintain the largest possible supply of ducks.

This co-operation is a recent development. Not so long ago, it was fairly common to see outraged bird watchers walking about the saltings waving white flags to keep the birds away from the gunners. Equally, it was not unknown for the gunners to discharge an ounce or two of BB in the general direction of the flag wavers. Plainly no good could come of this situation.

That the wildfowlers have been brought into line is a great tribute to WAGBI's officers, and particularly to its secretary, John Anderton, for wildfowlers are an independent gaggle who are more than ready to stick up for their rights, real or imagined.

On the conservation side, the Nature Conservancy, the Wildfowl Trust, and the Royal Society for the Protection of Birds, have been equally far-seeing.

* See Appendix III.

One of the most far-reaching results achieved by WAGBI came from their negotiations with the Crown Commissioners preceding the introduction of the laws affecting armed trespass. These laws made it an offence to be found on land to which you had no legal sporting access while carrying a gun. In other words, it put poachers on the spot.

Wildfowlers have always been under the impression that shooting on the foreshore, below the mean high tide mark, is theirs by right and therefore a free-for-all as far as shooting is concerned.

In fact, most of the foreshore in the British Isles is owned by the Commissioners of Crowned Lands. Under the Armed Trespass Act, then, anyone found carrying a gun there was guilty of an offence under the Act.

What WAGBI very smartly and sensible did was to negotiate with the Crown so that *only* WAGBI members would have the right to shoot on the foreshore. The Commissioners quite rightly saw this as a way of controlling the situation and placing it in the hands of an organisation which had a vested interest in making its members behave. WAGBI clubs appointed wardens. Most WAGBI members are in themselves responsible. If they aren't they find themselves expelled. With expulsion goes their right to shoot beyond the sea wall. The result has been that the foreshore has not become 'blown up' as it might otherwise have been.

Some people ask what they get from joining WAGBI. These are the sort of shooters who expect a material return including extra or free shooting. In this case, they get both. More important, in this issue as in many others, they received representation where it counts –

where opinions are formed and laws are made, in other words in Parliament.

WAGBI, as I have said, has teamed with non-shooting bodies to conserve ducks and geese, if only because to have more duck and geese means to have more sport. The aim of the conserving bodies, including WAGBI, has been, and still is, to set up a chain of sanctuaries around Britain where duck can rest unmolested. In many cases these sanctuaries are right on the edge of shooting areas, and in some instances the wildfowlers have actually been persuaded to give up shooting-grounds in favour of sanctuaries. Where this has happened the result has been beneficial to all. For the sanctuary has inevitably brought more duck to the area, and, since duck flight about in search of food and shelter, it has meant more duck crossing the wildfowlers' marshes where they become fair game to the guns.

The lesson from the whole exercise is that attitudes to conservation must be rational rather than emotional. They must always be based on a scientific assessment of whether a species is numerous and healthy enough to bear reasonable cropping. If it is, and the creature concerned is a proper sporting quarry or food animal, then let it be cropped in the right manner by people qualified to do so. And there is no disputing that the majority of wildfowlers *are* qualified. They have to understand their quarry and to be able to shoot well in all conditions of weather and light if they are to enjoy the smallest chance of success. On the saltings, at least, a winged bird is often not recovered (unless the fowler has a dog, as all good fowlers should); so, clean, and therefore humane, kills are essential.

On the other hand, if a species becomes in the slightest endangered, then all possible pressures, including shooting, must be removed from it at once, by law, until such time as it multiplies sufficiently to warrant cropping again.

It is up to all concerned to see that if the numbers do rise sufficiently to warrant shooting, then the bird is once again made a legitimate sporting quarry. That this will happen has yet to be shown. Meantime total protection of certain species has brought results.

Just take one case, that of the brent goose. This little sea goose was put on the protected schedule in 1954. At that time the species was at low ebb. Since that date it has increased enormously. Not even the building of an atomic power station at Bradwell in Essex has discouraged it from one of its favourite haunts. In Blakeney Harbour in Norfolk during mid-winter there are seldom fewer than a thousand brent. It could be argued that the numbers warrant shooting again. But the wildfowlers will, if they have good sense, resist the urge. They must remember this about most wildfowl and all grey geese, as well as black geese which means barnacle and brent: they are only in Britain for three or four months of the year. The rest of the time they are flying back and forth to their breeding grounds. Not all countries are as fastidious about protection as Britain. The numbers have got to be really well up before shooting is permitted again. There is the added fact that brent geese are not particularly good to eat.

Enough about wildfowl politics. Brent geese are not the subject of this book. Duck are. Thank heavens that no shootable duck are at present in the remotest danger in Britain.

THE BIRDS

What kind of duck can you shoot?

There are 247 different species of duck, geese and swans (in short, wildfowl) in the world. The British shooter is interested in no swans (they are all protected) only one black goose (Canada: the other two are protected, except that barnacles may be shot in the Western Isles of Scotland) and broadly speaking three grey geese. He *can* shoot fourteen different species of duck, which is not the same thing as recommending him to do so.

In my view, only edible duck should be shot, and this shortens the list considerably. An exception should be made where duck such as the sawbills (mergansers and goosanders) do damage to fishery interests, though please note that they can only legally be shot in Scotland. There they can be a menace to young trout and salmon. But heaven forbid that anyone should try to eat a fish-gorged sawbill duck. Other British duck very rarely eat fish, and then only fry, contrary to many people's belief. They live mainly off vegetation, plankton and insects.

The only other excuse for killing a non-edible duck is that it has been shot in half light. On such occasions, it must be admitted, there often isn't time to see the bird, let alone identify it. It's just a quick instinctive wipe with the gun and the best of luck. Obviously, if you are flighting where there are liable to be a number of protected duck (say shelduck) in the air, you will simply have to pause before you shoot. It also helps if you know that shelduck pinions make a characteristic and recognisable whistling sound.

Some doubt still seems to exist about the close and open seasons for duck, and I still meet inland duck-shooters who insist that they can start banging away on August 12. This date was done away with, and rightly so, by the Act of 1954: in August there are still too many flappers about – that is young duck that cannot fly properly – although admittedly there are plenty of the other kind as well. However, the season starts for everyone, shore shooters and inland shooters alike, on September 1, and not a day earlier.

Unfortunately the duck season does not end in quite such a tidy manner, and again the dates were altered in 1954. Inland – and the boundary here is the mean high-water mark made by ordinary spring tides – you must put your gun away at midnight on January 31. On the seaward side of this line, on what is legally known as the foreshore (in other words on the wildfowler proper's ground) you can continue shooting duck until midnight on February 20. The reason is that inland duck tend to pair and think about nesting earlier than their wilder and harder living neighbours on the coast. Let it be said at the same time that the same dates and demarcations apply to geese – bean, greylag, pinkfoot, whitefront, and Canada.

These, then, are the duck you can shoot within these seasons, and I put them under two headings, the edible and the non-edible.

Edible: mallard, teal, pintail, shoveler, gadwall, pochard, tufted, wigeon.

Non-edible: common and velvet scoters, scaup, goldeneye, long-tailed duck, merganser, goosander (the last two in Scotland only).

I do not include the garganey, which is undoubtedly both shootable and edible, because it is a summer visitor and shouldn't be around once the season opens. Then there are the protected ducks, including smew, eider, shelduck, ferruginous, and the occasional escapees from ornamental waterfowl collections such as carolinas, and mandarins (Surrey especially) which shouldn't be shot. This is where identification comes in.

Now for the duck themselves.

Mallard

Easily the commonest inland duck and occurring in numbers, sometimes in great numbers, on the coast. It is in fact *the* wild duck and is the only one entitled to that name. The term 'mallard' only refers to the drake, and is a corruption of the word 'male'; the female is the wild duck. The drake needs no detailed description. He is possibly the most handsome bird native to Britain when in full winter or breeding plumage. Most duck are identifiable by their speculum, or coloured bar, on the trailing edge of the wing. In the mallard this is an iridescent blueish purple. This colouring is not true colour in the sense that it runs right through the feather fibres but a coating which reflects light of a particular colour range in the spectrum. Usually, this colour bar will not help you to identify duck in flight since it cannot be seen from below. The gadwall, however, which has a white speculum, sometimes appears to have a gap in the rear edge of its wings, so perhaps the specula show up more in flight than we think. Flighting light is usually grey or non-existent, so possibly the other and brighter wing bars do no reflect well enough to show.

The mallard is a fine eating duck, particularly when coming off the stubbles in the autumn. Throughout the winter, except in periods of prolonged freeze-up, it maintains its weight and succulence very well. A big drake weighs around three pounds; a hen about half a pound lighter.

Mallard are dabbling, as opposed to diving, duck. That is to say they feed mainly by up-ending. They can

Mallard

reach down through 18 in. of water quite easily to grab feed on the bottom. They can also filter plankton and minute vegetable matter from near the surface with the fine sieve-like serrations on the inside of their upper mandibles. Favourite foods include grain, potatoes, acorns, worms, water insects and vegetation, seeds of many sorts, and occasionally very small fish fry.

They are good breeders and easy to rear. They lay up to thirteen eggs in ground nests, and, shortly after the breeding season, go into eclipse and moult. They lose their flight feathers and become grounded for several weeks. The sheen disappears from the drake's head as an aid to camouflage during this period. He also loses his vivid chestnut breast feathers and looks like a rather drab female. Often he has not recovered his good looks entirely by September. Most of the year the drake is silent, though he is able to raise a feeble quack in the breeding season. It is the duck who makes the familiar quacking sound, often heard contentedly in flight or raucously in alarm.

Mallard breed widely throughout the northern hemisphere. They are fine, fast fliers and are probably as quick on the wing, in level flight, as any of the duck. The wing beat is fast and stiffish and comparatively silent. My own guess is that a mallard is capable of 50 m.p.h. in still air, and that a teal, often said to be faster, does not do as well, at least in level, untwisting flight.

Mallard, if continually exposed to humans, can become extremely tame when on the ground or on water. The duck on the London park lakes are a prime example. Set them into the air, however, and they become as wild as any bird seen on a marsh. It is this dual personality that persuaded the mallard long ago to become the root stock of most of our farmyard ducks.

Teal

The smallest of our wild duck. They are found mainly inland, but sometimes in large parties on the saltings, where they are usually present in small bunches. Whereas the mallard tends to fly in pairs or in teams of five or six birds, teal are highly gregarious fliers. Sometimes twenty or more birds twist and turn together. They are tremendously popular with wildfowlers because, I think, they make extremely testing marks. I doubt very much whether they are faster on the wing than mallard. They certainly *appear* to be faster, but this, I feel certain, is largely because of their diminutive size and rapid speed of wing-beat. It's an old, old question which of the

Teal

two birds is the quicker. All I can say is that I have seen the thing put to the test once in conditions that left no doubt that both species were making best speed. It happened on a moor where some falconer friends were flying a peregrine at grouse with the aid of a spaniel and setter. The peregrine was 'waiting on' (that is to say cruising up top, waiting for something to get on the wing) when the dogs flushed some duck off a small flight pond. There were two mallard and three teal. The teal got away first in that bewilderingly rapid vertical take-off that makes it clear why the collective noun for a bunch of teal is a 'spring'. The teal 'sprang' and were well away before the mallard took off, quacking. The peregrine was now whistling out of the sky like a bomb and the chips were down all round. The teal appeared to be going much faster, to judge by sheer wing output, but after a hundred yards, the mallard, on slower wing-beat, forged ahead. No matter that the peregrine eventually stooped on, and killed, a mallard; it probably just knew a square meal when it saw one, or else the manoeuvrability of the teal saved them. There is no doubt which was the faster bird on this occasion.

Teal can jink and swerve like a trip of waders. They have a particularly testing characteristic as far as the gunner is concerned. At the first barrel, they almost invariably stand on their tails and go vertically up into the clouds. This frequently makes the second barrel far trickier than the first. A right and left at teal is something to put in the book. I think the moral is: take the first shot well out in front and hope that the survivors tower in front of you. Then the second shot is well on. Towering teal going away are for some reason not so easy. In fact, teal are never easy. When you pluck them in the kitchen you can see why. There is very little vulnerable target-area on them, though it must be added that one pellet put into this is usually enough to do the trick.

Teal present no identification problems, simply because of their tiny size. For the record, though, the drake is a beautiful bird with a chestnut head and greenish eye-patch outlined by a cream stripe. His breast is mottled with thrush spots and his flank feathers are vermiculated and much in demand by fishermen for tying the wings of Teal and Silver, Teal and Black and so on. The beak is big for the size of the bird and grey in colour. The duck is usually slightly smaller and is simply duck-coloured. Speculum in both sexes is a wonderful sheeny green bordered with white.

The drake makes a thin, high, creaking, broken whistle that can often be heard when teal are flighting at dawn to roosting grounds. They breed in most parts of the British Isles, the female laying eight to ten eggs in a ground nest that is often a long way from the water. Quite unlike the drake of other species of duck, the male teal often helps to look after the family.

Despite their size, teal are splendid eating; in fact I like them the best of all duck. They make a meal for one, with all the etceteras including bacon.

Earlier, I mentioned the vertical take-off abilities of teal. I cannot swear as to how they become airborne so abruptly but I have seen a slow-motion film of a mallard taking off that makes me think that teal use the same technique. The mallard simply spread its wings and pushed down until the wings were well below the surface. This shot it two or three feet in the air before its wing beat proper came into play. I'd suggest that teal do the same thing but go faster and higher because they are far lighter while still having a comparatively large wing area.

Garganey teal are similar in size, though slightly larger. The male has a pronounced white band above the eye and a pale grey fore-wing that can be seen in flight. The female is very like the common teal but has a pale stripe above the eye and a white spot at the base of the bill. But garganey are seldom present in Britain when the shooting starts. As previously stressed, they are summer visitors.

Garganey teal

Pintail

The pintail I think of as a coastal duck, although it does come inland and I have even shot one flighting out of a London reservoir. You often find them in large parties on the salt marshes. They are also present in large numbers when the Ouse Washes in Cambridgeshire are flooded.

The drake is a most elegant creature, having a largely chocolate head with a curving white stripe reaching up from the white breast along the back of the neck and turning in towards the eye. The speculum of the drake is bronzy-green with a brownish bar in front. The duck again is duck-coloured, though her mottled plumage is somewhat lighter than that of the mallard. However, she is a far more compact job and somehow looks pointed at the rear end although she lacks the splendid protruding tail feather that gives the drake, and the species, its name. Pintail are shy duck and fast fliers. In flight at long range the long fine wings help distinguish them from other ducks. They are rather gullible and can be called in with a mallard caller.

Pintail, all drakes shown

Pintails nest without much use of cover. They lay seven to nine eggs and occasionally cross-breed with mallard. They make fine eating.

Shoveler

Like all the duck so far described, shoveler are surface feeders, that is to say dabblers rather than divers; but they are dabblers with a difference. Their large spatulate beak is designed for sifting minute animal and vegetable matter from the surface of the water. Shoveler are not so common in England, but they are possibly the most successful duck of all, for their world range is wider even than that of the apparently ubiquitous mallard.

Though you find these birds on the coast, they are mainly freshwater feeders. Boggy pools, swamps, inland reservoirs can all hold shoveler. On the water the bird is squat looking and its head seems to sit low. This is undoubtedly connected with its habitual feeding attitude.

As I come to each species I find myself thinking that the drake in each case could lay claim to being Britain's most handsome native bird. The drake shoveler, apart from his Cyrano-like beak, is certainly an entrant for

Shoveler, all drakes shown

the male beauty stakes. His upper breast is white. His lower breast and tummy rich brown. His head is a darker green than that of the mallard, but it is the light blue on his wings that is so unexpected. The female is like the duck teal in colouring, though larger and with the same give-away bill as her mate. Shoveler often nest in reed beds. They lay eight to twelve eggs.

Though they tend to go away low when alarmed and are slower than the mallard, they jink rather like teal.

Shoveler can be good to eat though they are sometimes muddy. They are so lovely that it is lucky the opportunity to shoot large numbers seldom occurs.

Gadwall

These are comparatively rare duck, except on the Norfolk coast where they breed in numbers. The gadwall was artificially introduced there just over a hundred

Gadwall

years ago. On the private fresh marshes just inside the sea wall at Salthouse, near Blakeney, I have seen as many as two hundred flying in company with mallard and teal in September. Later in the year, when shooting starts in earnest, this population must get spread around to some extent. Certainly comparatively few find their way into the bag at Salthouse. I've shot them on the Ouse Washes.

Gadwall are somewhat mallard-like, though slightly smaller. Their wings are long and pointed which helps a little to distinguish them in flight, as does the white speculum previously mentioned. This shows well in the air, looking as if the wings have some flight feathers missing. The wing-beat frequently makes a whistling noise.

In general, gadwall are greyer than mallard, though this is only likely to be seen at close quarters. They are shy and easily put up. Gadwall like freshwater and nest in thick cover, laying the usual quota of eight to twelve eggs. They are good to eat but are unlikely to become a deliberate quarry of the fowler. They are, of course, dabblers rather than divers.

Pochard

Pochard are the first diver I have described. All divers feed by swimming beneath the surface. Diving ducks can go to an astonishing depth. Scaup, another species of diver, have been caught over 100 ft. down in the sea in trawl nets. (For the record: all duck can dive well, especially when wounded. I have seen hard-hit mallard go down and apparently never come up – even though I have waited for an hour, and come back again and again with a dog. The legend is that they hold on to something underwater, but I doubt this greatly. It seems more likely that they dive and swim underwater to a reed bed or other cover and lie just submerged. Possibly, though it is a nasty thought, they eventually drown – another argument for straight shooting and a good dog.)

Pochard are mainly freshwater duck but are seen on the coast, especially in hard weather. Identification of the drake is easy, since he has a rich red head, black breast, and grey back and sides. The duck is harder to spot, though she has the same flat, squat appearance as the male. The speculum in both cases is grey, although the female's shade is slightly darker. This bar shows up badly since it does not contrast much with the rest of the wing.

Pochard

These duck are very fast fliers, moving about mainly at normal flighting times of dawn and dusk. Most of the day they spend resting on open waters. The flight attitude is fairly distinctive. Pochard in the air appear stumpy, and, though they rarely call, the wings make quite a rustling noise.

Diving duck as a whole are much better on water than on land. This is because their feet are much further aft on the body, probably to give them maximum propulsion in and under water. This makes them clumsy walkers. They are also clumsy takers-off from water. They need a long 'run' on the surface of the water to get up compared with the leap into the air of the dabblers.

Pochard can be good eating. They build close to the

water, largely because of their dislike of long walks, and lay six to eleven large eggs.

Tufted Duck

The tufted duck has had a tremendous success as a breeding species in recent years in Britain. This is probably due to the increase in numbers, and area, of reservoirs. Big parties can be seen in London parks and consequently many people think of the tufted as a more or less tame duck. On the wing there is nothing tame about this bird. It is a fast and handy flier, and I have seen a drake doing at least 90 m.p.h. (admittedly downwind in a gale) on Hickling Broad.

Tufted Duck

The drake could only be mistaken for a scaup which has the same white flank and golden eye. The tufted has a very distinct nail to its beak which is shorter than the scaup's and its head is purplish (against green). The tuft is plain to see. Male and female both have broad white wing bars. Tufted are almost invariably found on deepish fresh water. The hen is a small dun brown bird similar in shape to the drake. She lays seven to fourteen greyish eggs close to water. Both sexes are remarkable underwater swimmers. They make good eating.

Wigeon

I have left wigeon until the last of the edible duck because, in the affections of most duck shooters, they have a very special place. They are *the* coastal wildfowler's

Wigeon

duck. Wigeon rarely breed outside the Highlands of Scotland, and the majority leave for the north when spring comes. They start arriving on the coast of Britain in mid to late October and are at full strength by late November. They certainly do fly inland to reservoirs, lakes, and flood waters, though mostly they roost and rest in huge packs out to sea. This habit of sea-roosting by many ducks, including mallard, is something of which the inland shooter is often not aware. Rafts of thousands of wigeon can be found two and three miles out to sea, particularly in hard weather. Once again, the Ouse Washes are of vital importance. Up to twenty-five thousand wigeon use this 23 mile long strip of floodland between Denver and Earith between the Old and New Bedford rivers.

The male wigeon is a most distinctive bird with chestnut head and custard-yellow crown. In the air he has a large white patch on the upper wing that shows up well. Both sexes have a white underbelly and pointed tail. Speculum in both duck and drake is black, green and white. The duck is an all brown bird with a very clear wigeon look about her. Perhaps the most characteristic feature is the neat, squat head of the species. The 'forehead' slopes very abruptly to the upper bill. Once you have held a duck wigeon in your hand you are unlikely ever to be in doubt about identifying another one. Wigeon are very recognisable in flight by their sickle wings and pointed tails.

The flight is fast but not particularly acrobatic. The duck has a not very musical *rerr-rerr* call-note but the male wigeon's whistle is possibly the most thrilling sound a duck shooter can ever hear. It is a high, clear, sweet *wee-oh* that is fairly easy to imitate. You can buy wigeon callers in gunshops, and you can make them by knocking the cap out of a 12-bore cartridge case and blowing through it. I once found that a toy dog belonging to one of my children, when squeezed savagely, emitted a perfect wigeon call through the metal valve in the bottom. I used it on the marsh with some success until the owner reclaimed it.

Wigeon are very much vegetarians. One of their favourite foods was once the ribbon-like green eel-grass, *Zostera marina*, which once grew fairly abundantly round our coasts. *Zos* suffered an almost complete decline in the North Atlantic between the wars. Other forms of vegetation (the rampant and rank cord or

Spartina grass is one of the culprits) are moving in on the foreshore. However, wigeon have found other food to their liking including sweet grasses and winter wheat.

Towards the end of the season they can, when shot on the saltings, have a salty taste. Many people describe this as fishy, though wigeon certainly don't eat fish beyond a very small ration of fry. Marine plankton and vegetation do give them a salty flavour, though, and when this happens they are not nearly as good as mallard or teal. There are things that can be done in the kitchen, as will appear later in this book. I have tasted many wigeon that were absolutely delicious. Those feeding on grass are as good as mallard.

These birds nest round rivers and lochs, and are late breeders. In Iceland they don't lay their clutch of seven or eight creamy eggs until June.

Non-edible Duck – the Scoters

These are sea duck, though they use freshwater in the breeding season. The drake of the common scoter is entirely black except for a yellow patch on the bill. There is a pronounced knob on the bill too. They have no wing bars. The duck is darkish brown all over but with lighter cheeks. The crest of the head is dark again. Scoters usually fly low, in wedges. A great deal of their food consists of molluscs.

The velvet scoter drake can be told from the common variety by the longer and more pointed bill with smaller knob, and by the white patch behind the eye. The duck is similar to the common scoter duck but with longer bill. Both duck and drake have large white wing patches. They are fast low fliers and exceptional divers.

Teal

Top In the hide at high tide
Bottom Shelduck, a distinctive, and protected, species

Common Scoter

They frequently go down to five fathoms and can stay under for three minutes or more. One sure give away: common scoters have brown legs; velvet scoters red, the drake's being brighter than the ducks.

Scaup

Essentially a salt water duck, but does visit inland waters. Superficially, it is like the tufted but the drake is much greyer on the back and appears quite light at a distance. He has no tuft and the head is black, glossed with green. The female is quite like the tufted duck but has a distinguishing broad white band round the base of the bill. Duck and drake both have greyish beak and legs. The beak is flatter and broader than the tufted's. Both sexes have a broad white wing bar.

Goldeneye

A sea duck, also but found on large inland waters. The male is spectacularly splendid, with black and white plumage and a purplish green head which shows a large white spot below and in front of the eye. The distinctive

Scaup

Goldeneye

thing about both sexes is the chunky, angular, as opposed to rounded, shape of the head. Unlike many divers the goldeneye doesn't patter to get off. They are swift fliers with a rapid wing-beat that makes a whistling noise. The duck has a brown head with white collar and her body is grey.

Long-tailed duck (protected)

Long-tailed Duck

A sea duck. There can be no earthly reason for shooting any of the sea ducks except by accident. The drake, long-tailed, is white and brown with a tail of at least four inches long protruding behind the body proper. The duck has a white face with a brown spot beneath the eye. The tail is pointed but not nearly so much as the drake's. The American name is 'Old Squaw'.

Red-breasted Merganser

A sawbill and fish-eater, which is protected except in Scotland. A large bird with wispy crest. The drake is pied with a green head, vermiculated black-and-white back and red legs. The duck has a horizontal crest whereas the drake's is in two portions with the lower piece hanging down. The duck has a pale chestnut head. In flight the drake shows a black fore-wing with a broad

Merganser, protected except in Scotland

white patch along most of the inner wing. The white wing patch in the duck has a black band nearly across it and parallel to the edge of the wing. The merganser eats fish, flies low and fast and takes off by pattering.

Goosander

A sawbill and fish-eater, protected except in Scotland. Though somewhat similar to the merganser, the male has no crest and a pronouncedly hooked bill. There is no chequering on the throat as in the merganser and the body is white touched with pink. The female is similar again to the female merganser. Her bill is like her mate's, her crest not so outstanding as the merganser's and her throat more sharply defined.

Goosander, protected except in Scotland

Smew (protected)

Smew

A sawbill and fish-eater which is protected. A fresh and salt water duck, it is far smaller than other sawbills. The female has a grey body and white head with chestnut crest. In flight the males appear all white.

Eider

A large protected sea duck. Both sexes are very heavily built, with a stout bill which continues practically

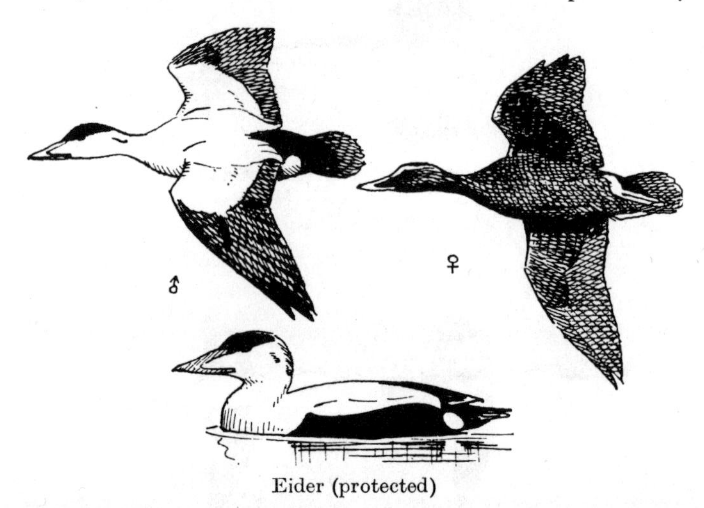

Eider (protected)

straight from the crown of the head. The males are black and white, the females all-brown. The eider is not likely to be encountered much by gunners.

Shelduck

The gaudiest of coastal duck; protected. It is large and said to be halfway between the duck and goose families. It is red-billed, with a chestnut band encircling the body. The male has a knob on its bill which the duck

Sheldduck (protected)

lacks. Shelduck are seen in great numbers on most estuaries. They appear black and white in flight at a distance.

Best advice: *leave alone anything black and white that is not obviously a tufted or scaup.*

THE WEAPONS

So much for the quarry. Now what weapons should you use to shoot duck with? I find that inland gunners are as vague about the right shot sizes for wildfowl as for pigeons. With the latter, the idea persists that you need something not far short of armour-piercing shells. Many people feel the same about duck, and possibly with more justification. Let me just say that the greatest professional pigeon shot in the country, Archie Coats, (fifteen thousand kills a year) uses sixes practically all the time, and sevens occasionally. He says that pattern is the most important thing, provided the birds are taken in reasonable range, that is to say 25–35 yards.

My own feeling is that very nearly the same applies to duck, *provided they are taken within sensible range*. Sixes are probably the best all-round shot size for everything except geese. The question of range is the all-important factor and there is something about duck that makes some gunners open up at quite fantastic distances and heights. At long ranges, small shot more often prick than kill, for there is some truth in the belief that a wild duck wears a bullet-proof vest; by mid-winter, duck have grown a thick coat of down under their breast feathers. However, within the 30 yard range sixes will kill any duck that flies.

But before coming down definitely in favour of any one shot size or sizes there are several factors to be considered, and they are all concerned with the type of shooting you plan to do.

First let us say that you are at the receiving end of the flight line. In other words you are at the point to which the duck are flighting to feed. Then, there can be no earthly reason for taking high birds. Even if they arrive high, they will usually circle before dropping in, giving you a chance that is well in range. My own choice when stationed round a flight pond or other arrival point is for sixes, or, if teal are expected, sevens. I go for pattern density, especially as the light fades, and I just will not fire at high birds.

Now for another kind of arrival point, this time a flooded field or a September stubble where cover is likely to be hard to find. Though the duck are determined to come in, they may easily spot you and swing wide at the last moment. In these conditions I'd take fives and sixes.

Next, we are not actually at the arrival point but somewhere on a flight light between resting and feeding grounds. Duck will be travelling fast overhead on a fairly straight course. They won't swerve, provided you are well hidden and the light is bad enough to screen the gunner. The weather and knowledge of local conditions is a key factor here. The harder it blows the lower the duck will be. Except in rough conditions fives would be a wise choice. On the Ouse Washes, especially towards the end of the season when the duck have been shot at a lot and tend to keep high, I often use heavy loads with four shot.

Change the scene entirely, and move out over the sea-wall on to the saltings. Here, for several reasons, the picture alters considerably. It is far harder to estimate ranges over flat open spaces like mud flats. Duck that look well within shot may just be in, but only just. Furthermore, duck have every chance of seeing you and swinging wide. If you've been waiting hours in a mud gutter and a freezing east wind you may still feel tempted to have a go, though I do urge you not to take very long shots. On the saltings, then, I would favour fives or fours and sacrifice pattern for range. Here, also, weather can play a big part in the height at which the birds fly and their ability to spot the gunner.

As far as one can make a general rule, then, I would say: for inland shooting settle for No. 6 shot; on the marsh go up one size to No. 5 and occasionally even to No. 4 shot.

Of course, the selection of armament doesn't end with shot sizes. There remains the question of the best cartridge and gun to take that cartridge.

If you mean to be a serious duck shooter, and I admit that by that I mean a specialist (either a coastal wildfowler or a man who studies the habits of inland duck as a pigeon expert studies pigeon), then you must have a gun for the job.

I believe that I've now had them all, including double four-bore, single four-bore, eight-, ten-, and twelve-bore game gun, semi-automatic, and 3-in. twelve, or magnum. The double four was not really a shoulder gun. It weighed 27 lb.; we fired it from a single punt, pulling both triggers at once with a leather lanyard and releasing 6 oz. of shot. The single four weighed, if I remember correctly, 16 lb. and was a hefty lump of scrap iron to tote out over the muds. It only came into its own once or twice at really high duck, and once at a spring of teal from which it removed ten birds. I'm a little ashamed of that feat in retrospect although it seemed exciting at the time. Nowadays, I'd rather hit one duck clean with a smaller gun than fire a salvo into a whole party. No, the four-bore is the gun for a professional – and there aren't many left – who is shooting to sell his bag. Even so I fancy he'd do better with a handier gun and less expensive cartridges. The only time that a single four can come into its own, surely, is against very high geese when using big shot. Then you may reach and kill where no other gun could score, but the opportunity does not often arise.

A double eight-bore fires 2 oz. from each barrel. This may seem a tremendous advantage until you realize that a 3-in. twelve fires a load of 1⅜ oz. When you take into account the fatigue caused by carrying a double eight-bore weighing perhaps 16 lb., and the lack of shooting efficiency this fatigue will produce, I doubt if the eight is a serious proposition – unless you happen to see one in good condition going very cheaply. A ten-bore should not even be considered; it has little, if any, advantage over the big twelve, for its load is only 1 7/16 oz. Again you may be tempted by a beauty offered at a bargain price. If so you can at least still buy cartridges for it.

The 3-in. twelve-bore magnum is as much gun as any duck shooter wants. It remains only to consider whether you intend to stick to the conventional side-by-side or to try the increasingly popular semi-auto.

I have shot on the saltings with several automatics and pump guns. I have once known an auto jam after being dropped in the mud. It refused to fire until it had been stripped and cleaned. A pump gun is far less likely to do this and, once you've got used to the trombone action by which you eject and reload, it is a fine weapon. If you believe that wildfowling guns should give you one choke boring and one only, then an auto is possibly for you. Personally, I still like the choice of two borings. Various adjustable choke devices fitted to the end of the barrel do permit variation of choke in an auto, but not between consecutive shots. On the other hand it is seldom that the five-shot or three-shot loading of the auto offers much advantage, for duck are usually out of range before a third, let alone fourth or fifth chance can be taken. If you can't hit them in two, do you deserve a third?

So I come down solidly and opinionatedly in favour of a conventional 3-in. magnum twelve weighing about 7 lb., as opposed to the 6 lb. of a standard game gun, but able, because of that extra pound and its enlarged chamber, to fire 3-in cases all day without giving you a severe headache.

If I was a better shot perhaps I'd also agree to full choke in both barrels, but I like to give myself a chance with the right, especially for teal in poor light, and so my magnum is bored half choke right and full choke left barrel. This is a personal view with which you may profoundly disagree.

Cartridges, too, produce some strong and highly personal views – though practically everyone is agreed when it comes to deploring their cost. There is, however, within the established range (practically all I.M.I.) a considerable variation in price and performance.

If you have a 3-in. gun there is no advantage in carrying the extra pound and a bit of weight around unless you get value from it; in other words, fire 3-in. cartridges containing 1⅜ oz. of shot. That they do kill at longer ranges is a certainty, as is the fact that they cost £2.25 more for twenty-five than the standard Grand Prix game cartridge.

But to own a 3-in. gun does not mean that you cannot fire other and shorter (and therefore cheaper) cartridges from it. You may get lead fouling in the cone or just outside the chamber but this is simply removed by the right kind of cleaning and anyway doesn't often occur. I repeatedly fire $2\frac{3}{4}$-in. cartridges from my magnum and find it does not suffer at all. I am suggesting that you should only ask maximum performance from your big gun when conditions demand it. Otherwise, it can become an expensive weapon. Waterproof plastic cartridges which have become virtually standard are a 'must' for the wildfowler.

Shortly after writing this chapter I shall be setting off to the Solway on my annual winter wildfowling holiday. There will be geese, but there will also be mallard, wigeon, teal, snipe, and probably a pheasant or two. With luck I shall fire a hundred cartridges during my three-day stay. I don't want to shoot a lot of geese, even if I have the chance, but for them I shall take a 3-in. Alphamax loaded with No. 1's and 3's. The bulk of my ammunition supply will be made of Hymax sixes. Hymax is a slightly cheaper, long range, $2\frac{3}{4}$-in. cartridge loaded for wildfowlers which I find particularly effective. The load is $1\frac{1}{4}$ oz. and the price around £4 for twenty-five. Maximum cartridges are a fair alternative to these; they are made for $2\frac{1}{2}$-in. chambers and carry $1\frac{3}{16}$ oz. of shot. The remainder of my stock will be $1\frac{1}{8}$ oz. game-load high velocity sixes which will be used on teal, snipe and pheasants. There will be situations at flight time when I shall load with Hymax in the right barrel and Alphamax in the left, though let me admit that this is not an ideal arrangement, since one has a nasty knack of using the wrong barrel for the wrong shot.

I have a sneaking feeling that cartridges are rather like golf clubs. You must have faith in them. If you develop a fondness for one type and one load you will probably hit things with it, just as you can always play a crisp No. 3 iron off the fairway because you like the look of that particular club. I feel that way about Hymax. From the first box of twenty-five I bought, I made eighteen kills on a wide variety of targets.

But then all that really matters is that you hold the gun straight and swing it at the right speed. Apart from the long range shots, one cartridge is very nearly as killing as the next.

STUBBLING

If you lack water on your shoot, you may quite reasonably decide that you will never see a duck on it. You could also be wrong, at least when the season opens, for duck can touch down on land almost as happily as they can on water – provided that there is something that makes the landing worth the trouble. That something is, of course, food – and food to their liking. Duck like nothing quite as much as barley, and even a combine harvester leaves a good deal of free feed on September barley stubble.

But a barley field after harvest is not much good on its own. There must be a source of duck from which candidates for stubbling can be attracted. Reservoirs, estuaries, river valleys, marshy areas, the sea – these are the places from which duck flight to find their food, and, if the stubbles are rich enough, a trip of twenty miles or so each way is not going to deter them.

I greatly favour the use of a 1-in. Ordnance map as a guide to duck-flighting possibilities. Close study of this will give a fairly good idea of the all-round duck-attracting possibilities. Provided, then, that you decide that your barley fields are within range of resting duck, the next step is to study the fields themselves. Are there droppings, feathers and, if it is a wet season, even foot-prints to be found? One mallard breast feather should be enough to set your heart beating a little faster. An evening or two spent hidden by a gate or along a hedge may well confirm your hopes. You may be very surprised at the numbers of duck which come piling in to your stubble field.

That the arrival of these birds coincides with sunset is the most important fact in the whole pattern of duck behaviour, and the key to practically all successful duck shooting. For the majority of the duck population, of all species, flight from resting grounds to feeding grounds at dusk, and make the reverse trip at, or just before, dawn. The ornithologists tell me that this is something imposed on duck by persecution, and that man is responsible for the fact that duck have become nocturnal feeders. I should have thought that large-scale harrying of duck by gunners and netters was a comparatively recent thing from an evolutionary point of view – in Britain possibly only becoming a really powerful influence during the last 300 years – and that it hasn't been going on long enough to mould the whole pattern of duck behaviour, on a world-wide scale. But such experts as George Atkinson-Willes, of the Wildfowl Trust, have in the past assured me that this is the case, and they should know.

For the gunner it is enough that this two-way traffic does take place and that he can use it to locate the duck and intercept them. Strangely enough the flighting habits of duck are again something of which most rough shooters are unaware. They regard duck as chance quarry, a welcome but unexpected addition to the bag. For these shooters duck are unexpected; what happens is that they occasionally surprise a few birds resting on ponds or in reed beds. For the wildfowler, duck are never unexpected. He may not see them because of some factor beyond his control, but he always *expects* to see them because he has worked it out that they should be there.

The duck which come in to the stubble field, then, are part of this evening performance. Their nightly visitations may be short-lived. They will last as long as the barley or wheat lasts, until the field is ploughed, or until something nearer to hand, more attractive or more plentiful, offers itself. Duck may keep coming, on and off, throughout September if the stubbles are sufficiently worthwhile. The problem now is how to come to terms with them.

Wildfowl have a well-developed sense of self-preservation, and so they will usually choose to pitch in the centre of the field away from all possible dangers. On a still night they will often circle around at a great height, particularly if they arrive in good light, to make sure the coast is clear. If they spot you standing out in the field – or worse, moving about – they will sheer off to another stubble, or at least not come in until well after dark.

If there is any sort of a breeze they will finally make their touch-down head to wind. As with all duck shooting, the rule is: the harder the blow, the lower the duck, so a stiff breeze is distinctly in your favour. In such a case, it is possible that you may be able to stay close to a hedge and take them as they come in head to wind and low enough to be within range. But in my experience this doesn't often happen. Even in a half gale they still have a nasty habit of shooting in high over the boundary and 'whiffling' down, spilling the wind out of their wings as they come, and dropping like lifts.

When stubble-flighting, the only answer, at least in

good light, is to make a hide out in the field. If you own the shooting, it will pay to build two or three straw bale hides, as you would for pigeon. Duck will not object to these and will accept them as part of the landscape.

If there is no cover, then you will have to contrive a hide that is as inconspicuous as possible. Camouflage nets on metal stakes are fine, especially if you can leave them up for a few days so that the birds get accustomed to them. Naturally, any hides need to be sited in relation to the flight lines into the fields, and the most used feeding areas. These you will learn from observation.

The trouble with permanent hides is that the duck may soon desert your field or, if it is sufficiently big, move to another part of it. Duck-shooting on the stubble can sometimes provide a very short harvest indeed and it may not be worth putting out bale hides.

I have had success with improvised hides made from nets propped on bamboo sticks or even electric fencing stakes. A net is a fair weight when garnished with stubble stalks and grasses, and so you will need plenty of stakes and binder twine to make the thing rigid enough.

If you're a wildfowler you will have learned to shoot from the most impossible positions. Lying down is one of them, for coastal wildfowlers frequently have to dig shallow 'graves' in the sand or mud to hide them from flighting geese and duck. The equivalent of a 'grave' can be devised in a stubble field by putting up on your stakes two nets each 6 ft. long and about 3 ft. apart. Between these two screens the gunner lies, prone, until the duck are right on him, then he sits up quickly and fires. If you make a hide of this sort, then siting it in relation to approach line and feeding area is vital, for you will only be able to swing your gun effectively in one direction. The proposition can be made slightly easier if you use decoys to guide the duck in as wanted. These should be placed about 20 yds. downwind of your hide and in the feeding area. I have used stuffed duck very successfully on stubble (in fact they were wigeon removed from a case of stuffed birds belonging to an aged aunt, and they worked very well – for mallard!), but solid or rubber decoys propped up as if feeding seem just as effective. Dead birds are even better.

Once the duck start coming, it is important that they see no movement. Quicker than anything else they spot the flash of flesh. Hands and face are certain give-aways. So, if you're really dedicated, you will have brought mittens, or even darkened your face and the backs of your hands. At least you must put on a hat with a wide floppy brim. A warning: don't use one of those camouflage veils if you wear glasses. The lenses steam up at the least exertion. Veils in any circumstances are an abomination. The best answer is to keep very still.

This is difficult, especially when the first party of duck come in. You hear them talking high in the sky and catch a glimpse of them as they pass directly overhead, out of shot. You're tempted to watch their progress. Don't. Duck seem to have rearward-facing eyes. Often you can see them craning their necks about as if having a really good look and this is just what they are doing. A spy hole or two in the hide is quite all right, though. They pass over nearly out of sight and then swing. They come back again, still high but possibly just in shot. Leave them. Let the pipe fill up first. These mallard want to come in, and that's a good sign. When the light fades a bit they'll be more confident.

You lose sight of them for several minutes and then you hear quacking on the ground close behind you. They've sneaked in, or perhaps another bunch has passed you, quite unseen. Never mind; leave them. They'll add to the attractiveness of the decoys. In fact, they are decoys – the best you can get.

The light is visibly fading fast now. Three mallard go overhead, low, their pinions hissing. That's duck for you. They can sneak past you out of an apparently empty sky. But where did they come from? They're suspicious. They climb away without landing and almost immediately swing across your hide. You sit up and fire. Miss with the first, miss with the second. Shooting from a prone start isn't easy. Now the original batch are up, but don't worry about them. There are plenty of duck in the air now, and they'll probably get mixed up with new arrivals and come in later, or land at once in another part of the field. You see two coming straight at you through the spy hole, and a long way off. This time you make no mistakes. You wait until they're nearly on you then jump to your feet and fire. That's far better. Perhaps this is the answer. Remain hidden and then totally reveal yourself for a shot at the very last second.

When dusk finally falls you can forget the hide altogether and stand out in the open. They won't spot you if you keep still. Duck will probably keep coming until it is too dark to see them.

As with all evening flighting the phase of the moon and the amount of cloud cover are crucial. The worst combination is a clear sky and full moon. Against this background it is impossible to spot the birds. A full moon covered by light fleecy cloud is perfect. The duck will be outlined against the cloud. There is a lot to be said for a moonless night when the duck tend to get in early. In bright moonlight they will keep coming long after sunset.

That's a stubble flight. How many did you get? Six? That's a very good bag.

FLIGHTING

The greatest single factor in the duck shooter's favour is the wild duck's inclination to 'flight'. Duck are nocturnal feeders and daylight resters. The essential thing as far as a resting ground is concerned is that it be as secluded and as safe from surprise as possible. The duck usually solve this problem by finding the largest sheet of water in the area, and then sitting out as far from land as is necessary for their peace of mind. Sometimes little parties will choose a small, undisturbed water, but in the main duck would rather doze the day away on a large lake or reservoir or on offshore waters within a mile or two of the sea-wall. Rarely do they find both food and shelter in the same place, and so it follows that they must flight at some time during the twenty-four hours. The movement from resting place to food is almost invariably crammed into the hour or so between sunset and darkness, in other words at Evening Flight. The reverse trip takes place in the hour which encloses dawn – Morning Flight. The duck shooter is therefore given the opportunity to place himself somewhere along the flight line between these two points. If the business of flighting was as simple as that it would lose much of its fascination. There are more variables in wildfowling, however, than in any other sport save perhaps fishing, and any of these can make the difference between a good flight and no flight at all.

I have already touched upon the business of finding a flight line. The first thing to do is to spot two termini – feeding place and resting place – and then to discover whether they are connected by regular duck traffic. This can only be done by considerable reconnaissance. If you see or hear no duck travelling on your first trip out at dawn or dusk, do not give up until you have made two or three recces at least, for a number of things can make duck desert a well-used flight path. They may come back to it later. When searching from scratch for an inland flight line the Ordnance map is as good a starting point as you will find. Let's say you know that the feeding ground is a marsh or sewage farm but you cannot get permission to shoot close enough to it. Then you have to find where the duck that visit it each evening come from. Does the map show you a reservoir, lake, or river valley within five miles range, and if so which is the most likely route the birds will take from it. Normally they will use the shortest possible line unless there are natural features to influence them. Such features include river valleys, water of any kind, a canal or even a continuous or partially broken chain of lakes and reservoirs, for duck would rather fly over water than land any day. Having discovered a flight line, the next question is: can you get permission to shoot along any part of its length?

Let's say that you succeed. You have roughly three choices. You can flight at the arrival point. This is probably the surest because the birds will be most concentrated and flying at their lowest and, sometimes, slowest. It's only fair to say, though, that this has one big snag.

The danger is that the nearer you shoot the duck to their feeding place, the more shy of using it they will become. For this reason many wildfowlers make it a rule that duck are *never* shot at their feeding place. From my own experience with artificial flight ponds, which I will discuss later, once a fortnight is the maximum frequency with which a flight should be shot actually at the point of descent. Shoot more than that and you certainly cannot expect big flights. Shoot too frequently, say twice a week, and you may soon see not a single bird arrive on a piece of water that once attracted fifty or even a hundred duck. There is only once exception to this. Choose a night when it is blowing a gale and little damage is done. The duck seem confused and are only anxious about getting in. The disturbance caused is minimal.

The second alternative is that you find a shooting position close to their point of take-off. This is a better bet in many ways, since duck tend to use the same routes out of a lake if they are going to a regular feeding ground. But there are difficulties here, also. If the roost is a large sheet of water like a reservoir, the birds can take off a mile or so from shore. By the time they come off the water they may be at least two gun-shots high, particularly if the water is in the middle of a populated area, or, indeed, if they have been shot at often. Duck very soon learn to recognize spots that often hold gunners. Once again the rule is: don't shoot too often, though you can afford to take more risks than at the arrival end.

Another snag is that you don't always know which feeding ground the duck are making for. Wildfowl are the least predictable of creatures. They suddenly find a better food supply, or flooding gives them a new ground they have never visited before, and the whole line of departure changes. Again, if you're the only gun out – and I stress that flighting is a solitary sport or at the very most one to be enjoyed with one chosen companion – a shift of wind may have pushed the duck off their usual line by two hundred yards. If this seems to be happening, and you see several early parties leaving on an unusual line, then take a chance and run to get under them, for it is a fair bet that for the evening, at least, the flight line has shifted critically.

Once again the answer is study and reconnaissance. Flight the place enough times and you will begin to know nearly all the possible combinations of wind and weather. Count no expedition a loss, for, even if you see few duck, you will have learnt something of value which may enable you to calculate the flight line correctly next time out. This element of uncertainty and the need to pit your own wits against the duck is the very essence of wildfowling.

The third possibility is to place yourself somewhere at mid-point along the flight line. This is the riskiest of all. Obviously any deviation of course on take-off is going to push the flight ruinously out of line by the time the birds reach you. In mid-flight they will usually be at their maximum altitude and will certainly be making best speed.

Though the same rule applies to all flighting, it is at least five times as important when you are somewhere along the middle of the flight path. The rule is this: the greater the wind and the worse the weather, the lower and more confused the fowl will be. Whereas on a dead still night it might just be worth going out close to the take-off point, and it would probably be worth flighting at the arrival end, it would almost certainly be useless under such conditions to try to shoot duck anywhere between these two places. The duck will be mere specks in the sky. The factor that makes duck fly lower in rough weather is that, due to friction, the wind speed is less close to the ground.

The variables that can affect the flight behaviour of duck are many, but some of the most usual ones can be listed.

Wind, rain, sleet, snow, and combinations of any or all of these will keep duck low and make them less wary. So will fog, though this often hides the birds from the shooter until it is practically too late. A gale is the best flighting weather of all – though, if the birds are moving downwind, they may be making anything up to 90 m.p.h. On landing, duck have to turn into the wind, and a gale when flight-pond shooting is very good news indeed.

Flood conditions can play the devil with flighting behaviour. Regular feeding grounds rapidly become unpopular. Stubbles covered with an inch or two of water, even grass fields in the same condition, flooded water meadows, reed beds into which a river has overflowed – all these suddenly become exciting new places to flighting duck.

Severe frost can be ruinous also. Duck soon discover when a favourite feeding spot has frozen in. They need a great amount of food to survive in cold weather and soon lose condition in a prolonged frost, for this reason WAGBI asks its members for a voluntary ban on shooting at such times. The duck hunt frantically for open water, moving from ponds to rivers, from frozen marshes to the old-fashioned type of sewage farm with natural filter beds (where bacterial action often ensures that the water at the top of the beds remains above freezing point). If the cold goes on long enough there will be vast migrations of duck to the open water of the coast. Nor need the thaw that follows benefit the inland duck shooter. Thaw often means flood, so the returning duck will have far too wide a choice of water to flight in numbers to the old freezing haunts. (Duck freshly arrived from the coast can sometimes be told by the salt 'tidemark' on their bodies).

The gale that befriends the flight shooter once the duck are in the air may betray him if he tries to intercept the birds close to take-off. On a big sheet of water such as a reservoir, a Force Four wind will whip up quite large waves. Duck get uneasy if they sit on a rough surface too long. They may either flight early, or move to an unusual part of the lake to find shelter – so that when they do come off they aren't on their usual line. Once again, close and repeated observation will pay off.

Finally there is the effect of moonlight. Duck flighting times are very largely influenced by the amount of light in the sky. On a moonlight night the flight may not take place until two hours or more after the usual time. Some duck may even be travelling back and forth all night. A light dawn certainly produces an early flight. Worse still, the moon is no good to a flight shooter unless the sky has a fleecy layer of cloud against which the duck are outlined. On the whole, then, dark windy nights and murky, blustery dawns are the ones to look for.

It takes a great deal of time to learn all the tricks that any flight line can play, and even at the end of two or three years of regular flighting you won't know them all.

I once shot a local flight line for ten years. To me its

fascination was that it ran through the middle of a built-up area. At one end is a reservoir and at the other a sewage farm. I controlled the shooting rights over a mile and a half of open market-garden country between take-off and arrival points. The biggest bag I ever had at one flight was five mallard and two teal. I suppose that on the average I made three trips out for every duck I shot, but these duck were worth ten on the Solway or Wash. Well as I knew this place, it could still deal me an unexpected hand. However I learned one excellent tip from it. It is this: if you have a flight line then keep a flighting diary.

Here is a typical entry from mine.

Dec. 20. Morning Flight. Blank moon. Out 6.30, in position 6.40. Wind moderate, south-west, slight rain. In position by single oak on river bank. First heard teal go by at 6.50, well to my right. Thought this unusual with this wind. Then a second bunch, followed by team of mallard (five, I think) just seen and on same line. New flight line developing, ran to get under it, caught tail end of flight. Too late for teal but got right and left at mallard. Only other duck seen after shot, one teal very high. Flight ended 7.05. Believe explanation of changed line to be that lights now go on in factory on other side of river bank at 6.30. Duck previously flew close to this. Do lights push them wide?

Subsequent flights proved that this was indeed the case. It just goes to show that it isn't only wind, temperature, food and weather that can change the habits of duck. Man can play his part, too.

The weather, then, is the main factor governing the quality of any flight. Ideally you should choose to flight only when the weather is rough, but unfortunately it rarely works out this way. If you live on the spot, then the matter is fairly easily adjusted. You go when the wind blows and leave the calm nights as confidence restorers for the duck. Most flighters, though, have to make their duck-shooting an expedition. They have made their minds up in advance that this is a day they can spare from family or work. Consequently, whatever weather the met. man sends they must accept with a good grace and make the most of it.

However, if you're planning a duck-shooting, that is to say wildfowling, holiday well in advance, you can stack the odds a little in your favour. For example, I would avoid at all costs periods of full moon. On the coast, when the wigeon are flying, moonlight flights can prove exceptional. However, the percentage of full-moon nights with the right amount of cloud cover is for some reason distressingly small, and an uncovered moon is useless. Not only will the duck come late, but they will be invisible when they do come. I agree all the way with what I heard a very famous shooting man say recently about flighting. In a dead silence at a rather sedate dinner party his voice suddenly boomed out: 'I like a dark night and get it over quick.'

Equally, if you're planning a shooting holiday which features flighting, there are certain periods of the winter when rough weather is more likely to occur. I have noticed, for example, that gales almost invariably accompany my own birthday which is on January 13. But this, I grant, is wishful thinking rather than dead reckoning.

Flighting is without doubt a separate shooting art, and one which defeats many game-shots at first acquaintance. Here, then, are some of the things I have learned about it.

First, be in good time. Get in position early. It's bad enough arriving late at evening flight but in the morning it is absolutely fatal. What on earth is the object of getting up at half-past five if you arrive on the flight line as the birds are going, or gone? You might just as well have stayed in bed. If you'd set the alarm for a quarter of an hour earlier you would have been nicely under them. Always, therefore, leave yourself a fair margin. If you arrive early on a dark morning, you can at least sit in the car until it's time to get into position. If you're racing along a country lane to beat the dawn to it you may yourself finish up laid out with the bag; roads can be very icy in the early morning. And it's far better to shiver for half an hour in your hide until the dawn does come up than arrive after the sky is lightening and the birds are moving.

For a morning flight, you can save time in the early hours by laying out all your gear the night before. I have driven my wife mad for years by placing a trail of clothes across the bedroom floor, first socks, long Johns, then trousers, vest, two sweaters and other unglamorous garments. The theory is that I can get out of bed in a daze and, simply by walking towards the door, dress myself on the way on the assembly-line principle. Gun, cartridges, hat, waders and waterproofs are displayed in a similar arrangement downstairs in the hall. When flighting at home, I reckon I can be in the car, dressed, gunned and dogged, and backing out of the garage within five minutes of the alarm going off. I stress that this is an emergency drill. I like to give myself a full quarter of an hour which allows for acclimatization, adjustment of body temperature and, most important, making a pot of tea.

When I'm going out in the morning I try to get up with the minimum amount of lighting. This is simply because I know I will see my first duck (if I see any) within ten minutes of leaving home. It will still be dark then, and if my eyes have become accustomed to dim lighting I will have a better chance of spotting a fast-moving target. For the same reason I stare as little as possible into my headlights and, when I arrive at the final half-mile of track which I know like the back of my hand, I kill my headlights and even douse my dash-board light. This may seem ridiculous, but I know my chances are going to be fleeting and that every little thing counts. The diary which I keep from year to year is invaluable in judging flighting times. I always note when I leave home and when it first becomes light, so I have a pretty exact indication of when to set the alarm on any morning of the season.

Now let's leave the morning and move to the evening flight, for which there are even more lessons to be learned.

Duck may start coming in full daylight in rough weather. This is especially true when there is a mixed flight. Teal will often arrive before the mallard, so, if you're out in the open, you stand little chance of connecting. Cover, in the early stages of evening flight, is essential. Very scanty cover will do provided that you stand still. Failing all else, if you stand against a back-ground such as a tall hedge you will be partially obscured from approaching duck, provided that you do not move face or hands. Face and hands are prime give-aways. So, incidentally, is a fidgety dog, and a fidgety spaniel is worse than a fidgety labrador for spaniels aren't well camouflaged. I've seen a springer stand out like a lighthouse on a full-moon flight.

In extremely exposed places I have, before now, daubed my face with mud from a creek. This is possibly going a bit far but on one trip it made the difference between some wigeon in the bag and a blank flight. Mittens take care of the hands fairly adequately, and the gun shops sell camouflaged pigeon masks (which I myself avoid like the pestilence). But I'm quite certain that standing still is better than all the additional personal camouflage you can devise.

Standing still means not moving your face even more than controlling your body because flesh reflects light like a flashing heliograph. And keeping your head still means not continually looking all round the sky for incoming birds. Just as when pigeon-shooting from a hide you choose your priority arc and then watch *that*, so when duck-flighting you calculate the direction of approach from what you know of the flight line and the effect of the wind upon it. Duck may flight in down or across wind but they will always land up-wind.

This business of not looking around applies to more than head movement; it affects eyes as well. The temptation is either to look all over the place, or to stare into the deepening twilight, focusing fixedly on one section of the sky in the belief that the duck must fly through it. Flighting duck have an uncanny way of going over your head without being seen for more than a split second before they pass. Possibly this is because you are close-focusing on what you imagine is the most likely area of sky. I believe that you will do better if you simply let your eyes 'soak' up the whole sky to

Top A fine sample of decoys
Bottom Mallard

A pack of wigeon overhead

A flock of pintail, even in silhouette this duck's elegant shape is distinctive

Above The wh
speculum is a
reliable
distinguishing
feature of
gadwall
Left A pair of
shoveler, note
unmistakeable
shape of the b

your front. Soak is the only way I can describe what I mean. This way, any object entering that wide expanse of sky comes to your notice quickly, even if it is not in sharp focus immediately. Having picked it up, you can then fix on it and identify it. I call this 'editing the sky' and believe me, it is a constantly necessary process. All sorts of misleading objects can swim into vision – homing rooks, carrion crows, peewits, gulls, gnats, spots before the eyes (which always move at mallard pace) and bats, especially bats. Pipistrelle bats have a nasty habit of looking exactly like jinking teal. Practice will help you to edit quickly, and it is vital that you reject the unwanted as soon as you have placed it, for it is usually while identifying a far-flung rook that a team of mallard knocks your hat off. Reject the unwanted quickly and return to an optical attitude of general focus.

Sound is a valuable aid to the flighter. Mallard frequently 'talk' on their way in at evening flight. The quacking is low-pitched and contented and can be heard at a great distance. So can the 'crik-crik' noise of teal. Pinion sounds help, also. And always remember that dogs have a wider hearing range than our own. Many dogs can hear flighting duck – and some can see them – before a man. If your dog is one of these paragons, sense when his head is beginning to lift to approaching duck and slip your safety catch off quickly and look up also. You may get a shot.

When dusk has fairly well fallen (but it is still by no means pitch dark) you can move out from cover, if there is any advantage to be gained by so doing. Duck will not see you in the open *if you stand still*. Why this should be so largely beats me, for duck have keen night vision. How else could they find their way into a flight pond between thick overhanging trees as I have often seen them do? How do they travel long distances across country at flight-time if they cannot very clearly make out the scene on the ground below? I think the answer lies once again in complete stillness on the part of the shooter. There are many tall, thin upright objects in the countryside – posts, trees, bushes. The duck whose eye is possibly fixed on the water on which he intends to spend the night does not pay undue attention to them.

Shooting from the open presents no difficulties, provided again that you do not put your gun up until the last possible moment. Then the duck is, or should be, dead before he has time to react to movement on your part. Never fire at long ranges when flighting if you are certain a closer-range shot will present itself. And while on the subject of range, never shoot at high duck which are circling a flight area while making up their minds whether to pitch. They will almost certainly make a lower circuit. To shoot at them will only drive them up or away altogether. If there are other guns out, they will be maddened by high shooting. If you're at the receiving end of the flight, wait for the duck to come right in before you fire. Duck travelling along a flight line are something else again. They're not going to circle and come back. They will travel straight past and so, if they're in range even though a shade high, there is a case for shooting at them. On the flight line itself, rather than at the terminus, such a shot may be the only chance of the evening.

Shooting duck from cover is exactly like shooting pigeon from a hide. You have a highly mobile target that reacts and takes avoiding action very quickly. Wait until the birds are right in to you, or almost over you, and then stand up and shoot rather than stay sitting or kneeling. Duck are fast movers and to hit them you need a fast, clean swing. Standing gives you the best chance of using your gun properly, but don't get to your feet until you feel the duck are practically on the end of your barrel.

Finally, do not pick up duck that are obviously stone dead until you are reasonably sure the flight is over. There may be more duck coming. If they see you or even your dog moving around they will be off to a fresh feeding ground for the night. Runners must, of course, be recovered and despatched humanely and at once. If it's a big flight try to remember where all your dead birds are for the pick-up. In a permanent butt you can, if you remember, place empty cases round the rim to record the directions in which duck fall.

INLAND FLIGHTING

More and more people are discovering the possibilities of duck flighting. Quite a few of these have not got suitable water on their shoots. Artificially made flight ponds are now the thing and, provided the craze doesn't get out of hand, they can produce very fine sport.

The two recognized ways of making ponds are bulldozing a shallow scrape in a low-lying piece of land, or damming a small stream so that the surrounding area floods.

Bulldozing is expensive unless you have a machine already working on your property. To begin with, you have to pay to get the bulldozer on to the site.

If you are damming, visualize what effect your flooding will have. Ideally, you want water that varies between three inches and a foot deep, with a wider stretch at the shallow end. Whether you are damming or bulldozing, your pond, if it is well sited in relation to a supply of duck, need not be very big. I have seen ponds less than the size of a tennis court attract great numbers of teal and mallard. If you are flooding suitable terrain you can afford to cover a quarter of an acre with water. The bigger your spread of water, the more difficult it will be to intercept flighting duck. If you plan the thing on a grand scale, though, you may envisage shooting it with two or three guns, in which case your larger area will be more effective.

When siting your pond, remember that duck do not like to be surprised. They appreciate being able to get early warning of approach. For this reason there is nothing wrong with a pond in the middle of a field. You can always give local cover by planting withies, sedges and reeds. Don't neglect wild food plants such as *burr reed*. Obviously it pays to scoop out a pool where water will collect easily and naturally. One pond I built refused to hold water (at least for some time). It was sited within ten yards of a river bank whose level was a good deal below that of the pond. The river was, of course, a natural drain and I should have known better. I had relied on the clay subsoil holding water for me – which eventually it did, but a pond bottom takes a long while to reach saturation point. Once the soil beneath is thoroughly soaked, it has a fair chance of holding water. Even so I had to pump water into my pool for a top-up every week or two. For a leaking pond there is one remedy, but it is expensive. This is to buy thick plastic sheeting and lay it on the bottom.

Though I have known fair numbers of duck flight into a small tree-surrounded pool, I don't think they relish close cover of this sort unless the area of water is sufficiently wide to offer them security. Build your pond small and build it in open country. After all, duck flight into wide open flooded fields with the greatest of confidence once the food is there to tempt them.

Hides for the gunners are an essential. On the more plushy flight ponds, there are usually sunken tubs with lids to keep the rain out on non-shooting days. (There is nothing worse than arriving, as I did recently, in short rubber boots to find 3 ft. of icy water in your butt so each tub should have a plastic bucket for bailing.) Rush or reed screens (hurdles, even) make good blinds, but a combination of sunken hide and screen is probably best of all.

Flight ponds need to be regularly fed. If there are a lot of duck, then a bucket or two of grain every other night may be too little. Just throw it into the shallow water and the duck will find it. Watch to see how quickly it disappears, remembering that moorhens and swans will eat it also. But if there are duck feathers about and your grain is disappearing, you can be pretty sure it's going down the right throats. Barley is probably the best feed of all, but any grain will attract duck, as will a sack or two of rotten potatoes, not to mention such trifles as acorns. Whole maize is an excellent food for flight ponds as it is too big for moorhens to gobble.

Duck like an island. Some moored straw bales, preferably enclosed in wire netting to hold them together, are excellent. So is an old door anchored so that it is just submerged. Feed can be put on this. Remember, too, that duck like an easy exit from a pond, so give them a nice sloping bank at at least one point.

The golden rule, and I cannot stress this too often, is to shoot flight ponds sparingly. Once a week is too often if you want really big flights; once a fortnight is just about right.

As I see it, there is only one danger with flight ponds – that we get too many of them. One flight pond in the right hands is self-regulating. Shoot it too often, knock down too many duck there, and the duck won't come again for a long time. However, near the coast it is becoming the fashion to have a whole chain of flight ponds belonging to a group of guns who then shoot the duck, in different places, far too frequently. This sort of thing could become a menace, though in the long run the situation probably contains its own remedy, namely that the birds will either leave the area, or spread themselves out in small and scarcely worthwhile parties between too many flight ponds.

I've been lucky enough to flight under many different conditions inland. You learn something fresh about duck at every new place you visit. Here are some examples of what inland duck flighting can be like.

The first example is flighting which takes place on one of the most famous duck marshes in England. This marsh lies just inside the sea-wall and in the middle of one of the most thickly populated duck areas in East Anglia. It is what I call a plushy pond – in fact several plushy ponds. In Norfolk, wildfowlers make a beautiful distinction between this kind of flight and one shot on the saltings. They call the latter 'a wild flight'. In many ways, this particular place produces a tame flight, always allowing for the fact that the duck are just as hard to hit. This sort of marsh has two advantages: (1) that you know the birds will be there, (2) that you have adequate cover and a firm footing from which to shoot.

All told, I suppose this piece of marshland occupies about one hundred acres. It is riddled with dykes, and the water level can be controlled. The owner keeps it more or less dry until September and then suddenly floods it so that it becomes a magnet for every easy-living duck in the district. Plenty of grain is then put down.

The main resident population, during the winter at least, consists of teal. Earlier on, there are plenty of gadwall and mallard. The mallard, of course, flight throughout the winter; and wigeon come in from the sea at flight-time in November and December, but less so in January (by when they seem to have cleaned the place out of the grasses which most appeal to them). Occasionally 'tame' greylag geese lope about in the dusk, though these are not shot; they breed locally and are treated more or less as pets. Over the sea-wall you can often hear the harsh but beautiful ringing cry of the brents. There are up to one thousand of them in the neighbourhood. They increasingly come inland to feed on young wheat. They're protected of course. Snipe, both jack and common, get up and zither round in the gloom. On a long fleet under the sea wall, goldeneye and long-tailed duck can often be seen. There are plenty of shel-duck, too, though nobody loves these very much for they are said to eat a good deal of the grain put down for the edible, and non-protected, duck.

Evening flight is the thing here, and, according to which flight pond you shoot, you can expect a preponderance of teal, mallard or wigeon. But you get teal everywhere; there are perhaps eight hundred in the marsh on a good day. Morning flight is generally only any use when there is a half gale, or better, blowing in from the sea. Then the duck stay in the marsh and move between the ponds and the flooded dykes and drains. On a fine, still morning you might just as well stay in bed. After a shot or two, the whole duck populace will be up and heading out over the sea wall to spend a quiet day bobbing on the waves. To show what a rough morning can be like, a friend, who is easily the best wildfowl shot I know, killed, during a gale, one hundred teal to his own gun between daybreak and midday. He used 230 cartridges. This, considering the birds were doing up to 100 m.p.h. down-wind, was not a bad average of kills per cartridge. It was disgracefully many teal, but the temptation to go for a century in such conditions must have been tremendous.

On the evening I am about to describe there are three guns out. Each takes a different pool. Some of the butts are sited round the edges of the water. Mine is on a small island slap in the middle. As the other two guns plod out over the marsh to their positions, teal and mallard get up and whizz round the sky. I do not fire at them until I see the others climb into their tubs. A fair breeze is blowing, not enough to make a really memorable flight but sufficient to keep the birds on the move.

The light is failing when the first teal comes over. He's a tall one and moving some. I wipe at him and sense that I am not in the same county. Now occasional shots are coming from the other ponds and duck are airborne constantly. Four teal come straight at me wavering and swerving as they fly. I take them too early at about thirty-five yards and they split into two groups and pass left and right. The idea had been to kill one well out in front and then get a second as they towered. Instead, a double miss!

Now three mallard from behind. I hear the pinions hiss and then the water creaming as they land. leave them there but keep an eye on them. They'll get up at the next shot. An easy single teal to the left. I drop him with a long raker and whip round on the mallard who are now up and steaming for the far side of the pool. A choke barrel of sixes drops the drake at forty yards. I wonder if this counts as a right and left?

The sky is darkening fast. The sun has gone and the cloud hides its reflected light. This will be a quick darkfall. Teal are shooting all over the sky. I suffer the awful indecision of not knowing which ones to take. After two wild swipes at long, wide swingers, I settle down and let the duck come right in. Three kills in a row. Better to wait for them. Now that it's getting to be true flighting light I am shooting better. This, I find, is often the case. When you've got bags of time to spot your duck, make up your mind, and fire deliberately, the result is too often a poke. See a fast-moving shape in the gloom, swing at it as a reflex, and it often comes down cleanly.

I'm so busy watching the teal that I completely miss five larger shapes until they are right above my head. The drake's whistle tells me they are wigeon. But they're suspicious and fly wide, coming back at last to head the wind and drop. I trim out two as they slide through the sky with paddles down and airbrakes set.

Nearly pitch dark now. A quick snap at a quacking form puts a lone mallard duck in the bag. The last shot is a stroke of luck. I hear wings whistling, pick out a single teal, and then he skims so low that I lose him in the dark line of the water's surface. But I can still see his reflection shooting in to land. I swing on the reflected duck, or rather just a little above it, and pull. The reflection becomes one with its owner as the little duck crashes stone dead into the water in a smother of spray.

I've no runners to search for and have a fair idea where my birds have dropped. As I remember it, I've seven teal, two wigeon, and two mallard. For twenty-three cartridges. Not too bad a flighting average. I pick up what I can find *without using a torch*. On a flight pond this is vital. Once it gets dark, the birds *must* be left to come in without a battery of flashing lights in their faces. Lights probably do as much to drive them away as has the earlier shooting. I gather nine of my birds knowing that my host will be round first thing in the morning with the dogs to pick up finally. He'll have to be early, for the gulls are at work as soon as it's daylight. On this marsh I've seen the blackbacks pick a mallard completely clean in the time it took us to walk back to the cars and have a quick breakfast.

Now for a completely different setting and a different time of day. It is December 20. I am at home. I have been away on business and haven't had a trip out for a fortnight. Tomorrow morning, I decide, whatever the weather, I must have a go at my local flight line. I am so out of touch that I do not know what time it will be light. So I get out the diary and discover that when I did a morning flight on December 18 last year, it was not properly light until 7.30, but that it was light enough to shoot by 7.10. From the same source I learn that the first teal came off at 7.05 and that I only heard them in the darkness. A further note reminds me that there was a half-moon low in the sky and still giving a bit of light when I arrived on the flight line at 6.45.

There is no moon tomorrow. The forecast is for wet, blustery weather. It should be ideal. If it's really like that, the duck will be inclined to flight late. I decide that if I set the alarm for 6.45 a.m. and am on the flight line by 7.15, I should be in time, at least if I go to the nearest flighting point.

Broadly speaking, my flight line offers two positions in the early morning. The first and most accessible is with a hundred yards of the water where the duck rest. If the wind is right, I then get the birds hurtling over me in the dark like driven partridges. However, this position has the snag that on a still morning the first shots *can* put the whole lot up. I have before now shot at a couple of duck and watched two hundred mallard and teal get up and wheel away while reloading. A dark morning and a bit of wind blowing from the water – as should be the case tomorrow – and all is well.

The second alternative is to flight half a mile further along the line on the river bank. This is a situation I discussed earlier. Here you will get better, faster, higher birds, and the flight may string out over a longer period, but, unless the morning is rough, the duck may be too high to shoot at. Another thing, if I'm going to the river bank, I must set the alarm at least a quarter of an hour earlier as I have to drive round by muddy lanes and then walk four hundred yards along the river.

So I go to bed deciding on the easier position. But in the night I wake to hear the wind rattling the windows as though it's trying to break into the house. My ears, I find, are peculiarly sensitive to weather noises in the depths of pre-flighting nights. I switch on the torch and reset the alarm for 6.45. That should do it.

The alarm seems to go off the next second. Drake, my springer spaniel, hears it and lopes upstairs to throw himself against the outside of the bedroom door in case I haven't got the message. I perform my somnambulist dressing act, making as little noise as possible, stumble downstairs and switch on the electric kettle. Five minutes from unconsciousness I am delivering a cup of tea, a peace offering, to my long-suffering and, I must say, understanding wife (God help a wildfowler who doesn't have a sympathetic and indulgent partner). A peer out of the back door reassures me that all is agreeably dark and rough. I take my time (two minutes) drinking the tea, put on my outer clothes, check that I have enough cartridges (for this job fifteen is the maximum I need) and climb with dog into the car.

When I get onto the rough track where the risk of meeting anyone is a thousand to one against, I kill my headlights and switch off the dashboard light. It is, glory be, blowing fit to bring the telephone wires down.

It is now 7 a.m. and by the look of it, it won't be beginning to get light for another quarter of an hour. I decide to wait in the car.

At last there's a crack in the east. I ease out, let Drake out, and load up. I creep carefully down to the river bank where I've been caught many times by a party of mallard. I'm caught again. About a dozen, I guess, get up with an almighty quacking almost at my feet. But it's pitch black. I see one flickering form and fire. I'm conscious of the muzzle flash but not of a falling duck. The report is instantly choked by the wind.

Now for the business proper. Some very nice calculation of wind is called for. I know where the duck should cross on their way to the reservoir but the gale is slightly across their course. I decide to pick a spot about forty yards to the right of their best used line. This puts me slap behind a tallish oak so that the duck, if they come, will appear to me like high pheasants in a forest ride. The advantage, if they come late in full light, is that they will not see me until it is too late to jink.

A frenzied quacking from behind tells me that some duck have got up from the river. Their objective lies on the far bank, but the wind is from me to them so they will have to rise against it. I spin round in time to see five mallard turning across wind, having climbed into it. Three are at maximum range but two are definitely on. The wind is getting under their tails and they are picking up speed. I swing as fast as I know how. The first misses and the second drops the leader. Drake runs in and comes back with a fine big mallard drake in his mouth. An unexpectedly good start.

While I'm putting it in my bag I hear teal on the wing. 'Crik-crik.' Very close. Too close. I catch five small shapes belting for home directly above my head. Their speed with most of the wind behind them? Certainly not under 60 m.p.h. But they were in range and that's a good sign.

A pair next, slightly to the left, and nearer to their usual line. Two clean misses. Far lighter by now, so I see the next big bunch as they clear the tree. There must be thirty birds and they are very high. I pull the choke barrel and to my surprise see a duck drop out. In the half light he seems to hang dead in the air for a long time, and his eventual parabola to earth seems to be almost in slow motion. I have repeatedly experienced this illusion with high birds in bad light. They appear to fly on, even though you know they are stone dead. The teal falls a good fifty yards behind. Another drake.

That's the main batch gone, but for the next quarter of an hour, one's, two's and three's appear at odd intervals. This is exceptional. Usually on this flight line it is all over in five minutes, but today, with the gale, the birds dribble on for half an hour from first to last. I get one more teal, a duck that shoots the hedge on my left side at head height. Three duck is as well as I have ever done on this morning flight.

And so back to breakfast greatly pleased and with that unbearable sense of self-satisfaction that comes with getting up early when everyone else has stayed in bed.

Drake takes a teal upstairs and offers it to my wife who is barely awake. She tries to look pleased. It is part of the ritual.

Another evening flight, this time on the receiving end of the same flight line. I think I explained that the feeding area on this make-shift suburban flight line of mine is a sewage farm. Let me hasten to add that the ducks travelling in and out of it taste delicious. They feed, of course, in the filter beds. By the time the water reaches these it is pure, though, of course, particularly beneficial to plant and insect life. So the feeding is enticing. There is, I stress, nothing wrong with what some of my ribald friends call my old sewer ducks.

The point about the sewage farm is that I am not allowed into it. Indeed, from a flighting point of view and for reasons previously explained, it would be a disastrous place to shoot from.

But it has this disadvantage. There is a 6-foot-high wire fence round it. Though this can be evaded by a tortuous and precarious route, entry into the forbidden territory is to be avoided for a number of reasons. One of them is the sewage farm manager. It follows, therefore, that it is a bad thing to drop birds inside the farm. It is almost a point of honour when we shoot an evening flight here that birds shall only be shot at which are certain to fall on our side of the boundary. We make mistakes occasionally and, since I personally hate shooting anything that is wasted, there follows, when this happens, the desperate business of lifting a dog and man over the wire and then getting dog, man, and (one hopes) duck back again.

This set-up produces some of the most acutely demanding shooting that I know. The birds (teal and mallard) are coming in hell-for-leather. They flight from the East against a dark sky. According to wind strength and direction they either come over high and then whiffle down in the centre of the landing area; or else, they rocket – teal do this especially – over your head, hedge-hopping; or again, if the wind is against them, they approach high and then begin that manoeuvre, wonderful to watch with wildfowl, of spilling the wind out of half-closed wings and dropping like lifts. In any of these instances they are diabolically hard to hit far enough out. Rights and lefts are something to put in the book here. Five duck is top score for one gun at one evening flight. But those five are worth thirty on the delectable marsh I described at the outset.

In recent years I have been lucky enough to become part-owner of a narrow strip of Ouse Washes. The washes run for twenty-three miles across Cambridgeshire and Norfolk from Denver to Earith. They consist of rough meadows intersected by dykes between the two artificial rivers built by Cornelius Vermuyden in the 1600's to drain the fens. One river, the New Bedford, or Hundred Foot Drain, is embanked and tidal. Flood water can be allowed to escape under control from this into the drains that run across the washes. The second river is the Old Bedford or Delph. Separated by three quarters of a mile of rough meadowland, this runs parallel to the Hundred Foot. It is not embanked so that when the flood water comes down from the Ouse catchment area of the East Midlands, the Delph rises and its floods spread out over the washes towards the Hundred Foot Drain. The washes are a safety valve therefore. Throughout the winter they can vary from being totally without surface water to being flooded bank to bank.

The duck population of this important piece of wetland is unbelievable – up to twenty-five thousand wigeon, eight thousand mallard, several thousand teal, the largest concentration of pintail in the British Isles with large parties of shoveler as well as tufted. Snipe abound while hundreds of the beautiful and protected Bewick's swans fill the air with their bugling calls.

You don't always shoot duck though you invariably see many thousands. As with everywhere else, the bag depends not only on your own ability to shoot from a cramped hide situation but on the weather conditions. On the washes, the weather is crucial. For a big day, the wind needs to be strong, northerly and to contain squalls of rain or snow. When the right conditions do come about duck sometimes flight in small parties up and down the washes all day looking for food and a quiet spot.

When I first went to the washes nearly twenty years ago, you could walk from end to end in the company of the shepherds who managed the grazing – provided you knew them well enough – and shoot snipe, pheasants or duck more or less as you liked. It was inevitable that the scene changed. Two things have happened.

A good many of the washes – an entire bank-to-bank is seldom more than forty to fifty acres – have been bought up by sportsmen. Large blocks of washes have been purchased by the Royal Society for the Protection of Birds and the Wildfowl Trust who have set up the most magnificent sanctuary, largely for the Bewick swans but incidentally for ducks, and built an observatory for its members.

Many wildfowlers were at first bitter about the arrival on the scene of the conservation bodies. Some still are. I totally disagree with this view. Shooting pressure on the washes is severe enough as it is. If there weren't any sanctuaries, the duck would have no place to rest in peace and would, I believe, rapidly decrease in number. They would go somewhere else.

Nor can duck stay in a sanctuary for ever. They like to rove around, moreover they need to – in search of food. Even a five hundred acre reserve cannot indefinitely provide natural food for perhaps twenty thousand ducks and swans. So the wildfowl flight out over the washes and the gunners get their fair share. I know there are some who do not agree with this view. They believe it is only a question of time before the whole of the washes are taken over by an Act of Parliament as one big reserve. I do not think that this is possible or likely. The present balance seems to me to be an adequate and satisfactory one.

Because I do not live on the spot, my trips to the washes, usually with two fowling companions, have to be planned well in advance. We must take a chance on the weather. About one in three times, we strike it lucky. Many of the locals just shoot morning or evening flight. But then they can afford to. We prefer to go out before light, set up hides in the dark where we judge the flight line will be and shift almost immediately if we find we have judged it wrongly.

Being able to move quickly is the key to success. The flight line on the washes is critical. Sometimes a matter of thirty yards will put you out of the shooting. I have known three gunners to sit twenty yards apart on a really rough and productive day, yet one of those guns has had most of the shooting.

The ideal hide on the washes is a tub sunk in the ground. This calls for a great deal of work and also a great many tubs to cover the flight line. The water table is only inches below the surface and the peaty soil of the washes simply squeezes out any unsecured butt sunk in it. Close season excavations are necessary to chain tubs down to anchors of crossed railway sleepers. Something of this kind is necessary to keep the tubs below ground level.

Any hide that sticks up above the level of the land is not ideal. Wash duck soon associate squat vertical structures with danger. You can watch parties of wigeon flighting down the wash climb as they cross such danger points. Yet we have little choice but to use portable hides. My own answer to the situation is a lightweight affair that rolls up like a carpet. I once used chicken wire but now I employ Netlon, that heavy plastic mesh sold as instant garden fencing. Through this I weave Norfolk reed (*Phragmites*) or even straw. One of my earlier hides relied on dried bamboo foliage from my garden. This dries a very suitable reed-like yellow and provided it is thickened up with reed or straw occasionally, will last a couple of seasons. Such a hide is also ideal for pigeon shooting.

Wired to, or threaded through, the Netlon are up to six lightweight stakes. Don't use bamboo poles if you can help it as they are liable to break and splinter, sometimes with painful results, when you are trying to push them into firm ground. On the washes this does not, of course, apply. The ground never is firm. Just the same I prefer something stronger and nowadays I staple the stakes sold as rose supports to the hide. I do not recommend camouflage nets. They blow about in high wind, make a noise and are distracting both to shooter and to duck.

You need fifteen or sixteen yards of Netlon. Once made, the hide rolls up tightly so that it can easily be carried under the arm. It is light and does not become heavy even when wet through. Its great virtue is that it can be set up in seconds. You can pack up, run fifty yards and set it up again in two or three minutes, an invaluable asset when you discover you are just off the flight line as daylight breaks.

The hide must not be more than four feet high and it helps if the top layer of vegetation contains some seed heads or leaves that can be pulled above the Netlon once you are in position. These break up the hard outline. Gaps should be made so that you can see through, not *over* the hide. Your seat needs to be low, not more than eighteen inches off the ground. Camp stools sink into the ooze and topple over. Squat oil cans are quite good and plastic buckets are not impossible. Some of your shooting will be done off your knees and very little off your feet.

On the washes, decoys help a good deal, especially if there is flood water in front or behind you. However, I have decoyed wigeon very successfully on to grass when using dead birds combined with plastic decoys and calling with a wigeon whistle. I remember this working best in fog.

Wash duck tend to fly high, so let the wigeon, especially the passing parties, fly almost over the top of your hide before you shoot. The second shot is always tricky, since the birds tilt upwards, using the wind on their flattened breasts to flare away.

For the rest, the same rules apply as everywhere else. Take warm clothing and a Thermos of soup. I use standard game load No. 6 shot in my right barrel and something heavier in the choke, say Hymax No. 4 or No. 5. On rare occasions I take magnum loads though the expense is not usually justified and I find the recoil of near vertical shooting excessive at the end of a long day.

We rarely stay for evening flight. I have never found it very rewarding. On perhaps one day a season the bag is a deep-freeze filler. For the rest, ten or twelve duck and some snipe between two or three guns, is a good day. Win or lose, or even score a blank, the Ouse Washes are a magnificent place to be. At the end of the day you will have seen a thrilling number of fowl and will have been completely cut off from the workaday world. The washes are, alas, privately owned, although there are one or two that advertise shooting. The Fenland Wildfowlers, a WAGBI club, has an excellent wash for its members.

PUNTING

Without any doubt the hardest way to shoot duck, let alone a lot of duck, is with a punt and punt-gun. You won't find many inland shooters who will believe this. Mention punt-gunning and all they will say is: 'sheer murder'. Personally I've passed through the punt-gunning stage. This is not because I think it *is* murder but because I am certain you need to put in an awful lot of time to be successful at it. You need at least a solid fortnight in the hardest possible weather and this, for most people, means arranging to take the annual holiday, alone, in January or February. Once you are married this is not likely to prove popular.

Punt-gunning is rather like salmon fishing. You must either give a block time to it during which the conditions, if they obey the law of averages, must at some time be right; or else, as in salmon fishing, you must live by the water and just venture out when river and atmospheric conditions, generally, are at their best. But I will return to punting proper in a moment. First I'd like to discuss boats in general, in connection with duck shooting.

I used to shoot on a coastal marsh – the one I described in the opening chapter – where a boat was an absolute must. This was because, unless you were prepared to maroon yourself on an island for the best part of six hours, you were always falling back ahead of the tide and, of course, ahead of the best shooting.

Our first experiments were with a Government surplus R.A.F. rescue dinghy. This was a fighter pilot's effort and consequently a one-seater, or rather a one-lier. Once you were in the thing, dolled up in your waders and fowling gear, you felt like a very fat man trapped in a close-fitting hip bath. Our idea was to use it, not for navigation in open water, but for crossing deep creeks on the way out to morning flight, when the tide was dropping but not dropping fast enough. Equally, we wanted it for the return journey when we had left things just a shade too late on a flowing tide and found ourselves faced with creeks too deep to wade.

The first time the two of us took it out (the other gunner was Richard Arnold) we had a very nasty experience in a deep and sticky gutter down which the tide rushed at an appalling rate on its way out into the North Sea. For some reason Arnold, whose dinghy it was, had brought a pair of coal shovels for paddles. I suppose he had only bought the dinghy that day and hadn't had time to get the real thing. Coal shovels proved completely useless in a 6-knot tide and Arnold was swept swirling down the creek towards the dark ocean. What was worse he was so trapped in the thing that he couldn't sit up sufficiently to grab the sides of the gutter and stop his progress. Ultimately he grounded when well down the marsh, but he was considerably shaken. After that we attached a piece of cord to either end of the dinghy and pulled ourselves across in a fairly safe and sensible way.

The dinghy had other disadvantages. For example, although it was collapsible, we never had time or energy to collapse it. Thus, having crossed a creek, we stumbled over the saltings with it draped across our backs rather like the coracle fishers of the Teifi. Coracle fishers probably have their troubles but they can be nothing compared with the blow with which a north-east gale can strike you when you are carrying an inflated rubber dinghy.

In the end we did master it and indeed got some use out of it. It made a first-class (theoretically) waterproof and mud-proof hide when dug in on the mud flats. But by that time it was generally full of water and mud on its own account, so it is doubtful if we gained much in the way of comfort from it. However, it did make a fairly stable 'grave' in which to lie and at least you did not sink further into the mud once you were inside it. It did, of course, only give shelter to one gunner and it wasn't the easiest possible hide from which to shoot.

On a flowing tide the dinghy had its points. You could get in it when the water first made up a lagoon or creek and allow yourself to be floated back towards the sea-wall. You knew you were safe from disappearing out to sea when coming in on the flow, and birds certainly rocketed all round you. You missed most of them, however, because of the impossible shooting position. It wasn't easy to retrieve the fallen because the dinghy was not really navigable, and certainly little headway could be made against the tide.

The next step was a canvas canoe. This, too, was a single-seater and, though an improvement on the rescue dinghy, never gave one a great feeling of security. It was useful for getting out to the furthest islands on the marsh, but you had to wait to float the canoe until the water was nearly at the sea-wall, and so a great deal of the mobility the rubber float had given us was lost. The canoe was retired when I ran into an iron stake in 4 ft. of very cold water and ripped a 6-in. gash in the bottom. If the water had been any deeper, and if the tide had been making instead of ebbing, the results might have been fatal. Waders full of water render you almost helpless.

About this time I decided to build a marine plywood dinghy for fishing. This was of the type you can put on top of your car, but it still needed two fairly strong men to carry it any appreciable distance. It had the same snag as the canoe, namely that you had to wait for nearly full tide before you could float it. Unlike the dinghy, it was so tough that you could safely leave it anchored halfway out on the marsh in the stormiest weather. This enabled you to walk out long before the tide reached the wall and gave, in ideal conditions, perhaps an extra two hours of good shooting. Since we didn't live close to the marsh, we had, at the end of every excursion, to bring it back to the wall again. This meant coming in on the flood and often packing up when the shooting was at its best.

The good thing about all these experiments was that it enabled us to learn a great deal about boats, and the reactions of birds to boats, under marsh conditions. The next stage, obviously, had to be a full-blooded gunning punt.

Punt-gunning is at least as old as flintlocks. There are very early prints of Fen gunners dragging themselves along on the ice on heavy sleds, on which are mounted cannon-like flintlock fowling pieces. In each hand they hold a sort of ice dagger with which they gain purchase. Presumably the flocks of fowl were not nearly so wild in those days, and in extremely cold weather they may even have been quite approachable. It isn't my experience that they are either trusting or approachable these days and I am certain other punters will agree with this.

Far from being 'murder', as the rather smug covert shooter declares it to be, punting is a great skill, the excitement coming from the stalk rather than the shot. In fact, the shot does not materialize all that frequently, and when it does the pick-up is often very slim indeed. The picture of hundreds of duck falling dead on the water from an unsporting 'sitting' shot is very far from the truth. It is true that there are occasional shots of

PUNTING IN THE OLDEN TIME.

Early fenland punter with massive flint lock solidly fixed to boat. Note white clothing. Dog appears to be an Irish Water Spaniel

seventy-five wigeon and there is on record at least one recent shot of 105 teal. But then the gunner who made this had been punting for three weeks without a decent bang. He probably didn't make another shot of any sort for a week or two. Moreover, he was a professional shooting for his living.

Nowadays punt-guns are practically all breech-loaders. They should be, anyway. Any muzzle-loader that comes your way is probably not safe to shoot, for it must be at least sixty years old. Many shot-guns of this age are as sound as the day they left their makers but punt-guns have to endure awful conditions of salt and rust and muzzle-loaders were rarely cleaned properly. If you are tempted to buy one for a few pounds, for heaven's sake have it sent to Proof before you use it, and, if it passes, fire small charges from it afterwards.

The biggest gun that the law now permits is one with a maximum bore of 1¾ ins. This was laid down by the 1954 Protection of Birds Act. It still allows the gunner plenty of latitude. A gun of this size will probably throw a charge of 22 oz.

Such a gun will normally have a screw breech and will be fired by a lanyard. It will almost certainly be single-barrelled, though a few classic 'doubles' have been made. The great Colonel Peter Hawker, father of modern shooting, built the most famous of these and it can be seen today in the Museum of the Birmingham Proofhouse. The right barrel is fired by percussion lock and the left by flint, the idea being that there would be a slight hang-fire on the second barrel to catch the survivors with wings open as they sprang after the first barrel. Sir Ralph Payne-Galwey had a double, too (see illustration), but this was later, I believe, split into two guns.

A big single, throwing a pound of shot, will probably weigh between 80 and 100 lb. Even so it recoils quite a bit. In the past, various spring recoil-absorbers have been tried, but the safest and most usual method of taking the shock of discharge is by a breeching rope passed round, or through, the butt of the gun and running forward to pass through the stem block of the punt. The whole punt thus takes the shock and moves backwards appreciably through the water on firing.

A big gun like this needs a double punt. In this, both punters lie prone, the gunner propped up behind his piece and the sculler, or 'setter', lying behind him. The latter has the gunner's feet in his face and he must provide propulsion by operating a long whippy scull over the starbard quarter. This is an art in itself, and teamwork between the two men needs to be very close for success.

Amateur punters – there are few professionals left – tend to use far smaller rigs these days. A much handier

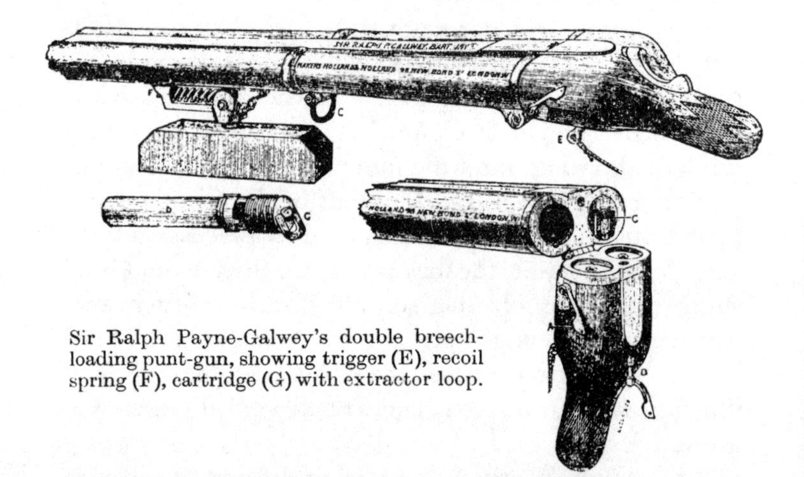

Sir Ralph Payne-Galwey's double breech-loading punt-gun, showing trigger (E), recoil spring (F), cartridge (G) with extractor loop.

gun is a 6 oz. weapon such as that once made by Thomas Bland Ltd. of 21 New Row, off St Martin's Lane. Blands have always catered for wildfowlers, both shoulder- and punt-gunners. The Bland 6 ouncer is a screw breech weapon that fits very nicely into a light single-handed punt.

Single punting is equally exacting, for here the gunner is his own navigator. In some cases he may choose to scull, though his boat probably offers little room for this. If the water is shallow enough he may push himself along with setting poles. When it comes to the close approach for the shot, he will probably have to abandon these, or rather bring them quietly inboard, and make the last vital hundred yards with hand paddles over each side of his cockpit. This may call for him to keep his hands and wrists in icy water for up to forty minutes. After that, let's hope he has sufficient circulation left to pull the string.

The traditional colour for all fowling boats is kittiwake grey. This hasn't come about by accident. In moonlight, or in a dawn drizzle against mud banks, grey is the colour that gives least chance of detection. Any visible parts of the punter's clothing, particularly his cap, should be of this colour or off-white.

Double punts are often taken well out into open water, sometimes a mile offshore. This means that the users must be pretty good boatmen and understand weather signs. Plenty of punters have been lost by failing to read the weather correctly, and many a big gun has been tipped over in deep water to save craft and crew. For this reason, most big gunners attach a float by line to the gun in case they should ever have to ditch. Single punters are well advised to operate in sheltered waters, for their boats must be narrow in the beam if only so that they can operate hand paddles comfortably on either side of the cockpit.

When it comes to cartridges, punters 'roll their own'. The basic requirements are: coarse-grained black powder (you can buy it from any gunsmith provided you have a licence from the Chief Constable of your area); brass cartridge bases, machined for your gun; .32

automatic blanks which are used as primers; shot, usually BB's and certainly not smaller than No. 1; tow and card for wadding; and cardboard tubes (made by Spicers) which are stuck on the brass base to form the cartridge case. It pays to make up only a few at a time. Indeed, you will never need more. Cartridges have a nasty habit of deteriorating in salt atmosphere, and half a dozen is the maximum you need in your magazine at any one time.

The magazine is a useful accessory, not only for storing ammo, tools, and lubricants but also, if made with a sloping lid, for use as a prop to the chest for the gunner when lying behind his piece.

There are other essential pieces of equipment. I strongly advise against wearing waders in a punt in case of an upset. Old boots or even plimsolls are best. They should be lace-ups, anyway, but with lacings that can be kicked free in emergency. The accessory needed to make these usable once you get out of the boat and on to the quaking muds are 'splatchers' or mud patterns. These are flat, stout footboards with rope attachments. You slip the ropes over the toes and round the heels of your boots or plimsolls, so that you can cross the morass. This is frequently necessary for picking up birds on a dropping tide or even for walking home when you have misjudged things and been left high and dry.

You need, too, a very old but sound 12-bore, probably a cheap single-barrelled gun. This is for knocking out quickly and mercifully any wounded birds after a shot. In the old days this was called a 'cripple-stopper'. I must admit that I dislike the term and its implications. Probably you just have to come to grips with the idea that punting doesn't kill every bird outright, but then nor does shoulder-gunning. Certainly you must carry such a weapon, preferably on racks beneath the coaming or under the foredeck if there is room. There it will escape the worst of the spray. It should go without saying that this gun must never be kept loaded in the boat. Just the same, I have heard of quite a few gunners blowing the bottom out of their punts by failing to observe this obvious safety rule.

Many other items such as compass, waterproof sheet, Thermos, food and extra cordage are optional, but an anchor is not. Sooner or later you are bound to have to leave your boat because you have misjudged the tide. A light mud anchor is probably the best answer, but make sure you have more rope on it than the maximum expected rise of tide.

Conditions of poor visibility are usually the best ones for punting. That and intense cold when fowl have left frozen inland waters. Unfortunately, the punter can rarely take advantage of the gale that helps the shore gunner. For one thing his boat wouldn't live in it, and, even if it did, it would present far too unsteady a gun platform. You can punt in moonlight, dawn-light or mist and expect fair results. Sometimes if you are extremely lucky or skilful you can get close enough to fowl in broad daylight, but the occasions are rare.

Wigeon are the punter's main quarry. Brent geese, of course, used to be too before they were protected. Occasionally nowadays, particularly in Southern Ireland, the punter may get a shot at grey geese on the sea but they are pretty wary. Duck other than wigeon, especially mallard, are sometimes found well off the coast. Mallard are very tricky and often rise at too long a range with a great quacking that warns everything else in the neighbourhood and puts the wigeon flocks into the air as well. A big raft of wigeon with a few mallard outriders presents a very nasty problem. Almost certainly the mallard will spoil the chance of a good shot.

In the enclosed waters of the creeks you may meet anything, though probably in smaller numbers. Pintail, shoveler and teal are all possibles as well as the more usual mallard and wigeon.

Now to reconstruct a punting expedition.

It is early morning. Let's say that you are dropping down an estuary as the tide ebbs. The gun is loaded and the sculler is sitting upright at this stage, probably rowing with short sculls or paddling. The gunner is searching for'ard for birds with his glasses.

He reports that some wigeon have dropped in about half a mile ahead. Just one bunch at first and then two more parties. Almost certainly there is a big party building up on one of the sand bars. There is still a long way to go but at about a quarter of a mile, when still hidden from the duck by a bend, punter and gunner get down into action stations. The punter has his long scull out and, though the current is taking him down quite fast, he uses it to drive forward; for, on a dropping tide, there may not be much time left to get close to the birds.

They round a corner in the creek and the gunner kicks the punter quietly in the face. This is painful but is a recognized signal between them. It means that the gunner has sighted the quarry. The punter raises himself slightly and squints over the gunner's shoulder. In the bad light he can just make out a dark mass on the shoulder of a sand bar. He can see some dots swimming

The late Jeffery Harrison putting out decoys in a tidal gutter amid the ice on a cold morning

A mixed flock of teal, mallard and gadwall

in the water at the edge of the sand. Wigeon. At least a hundred of them. He immediately brings the punt round so that the knife-edge bows are facing the duck and the boat presents its least visible aspect to them. Now he lets the current do most of the work and uses the scull to keep direction. He has quite a struggle, for the stream is trying to swing him across the river so that the side of the punt will show to the birds. He is still squinting over the gunner's shoulder with his head slightly raised. Two hundred yards to go. They need to be within sixty for a decent chance of a shot, and they certainly shouldn't fire at much over seventy.

The birds are still undisturbed. The punter is flattened now. He can't see much at all and he daren't raise himself to look. The gunner is navigating by tapping him, more gently now, first with his left foot for more left 'rudder', then twice with his right for violent right correction.

The gunner is trimming the elevation of his gun now so that he can come to bear at maximum range. To do this he operates a long rod like a billiard cue rest. The rest part is under the barrel of the gun, well down the sloping foredeck. The handle of the rest reaches back into the cockpit. It follows that if the gunner pushes the rest down the sloping foredeck the muzzle will depress; if he pulls it up the gun will elevate. Crude but effective.

The duck are still sitting nice and thick. It looks like a good shot. Should be fifty wigeon at least. Then there is an awful rasping sound under the boat. The tide has dropped too fast. The punt is touching bottom. The punter shoves desperately and they're off again. Eighty yards. The gunner's heart feels as though it will stove a hole in the bottom planks. At seventy yards they stick again and, before the sculler can check it, the punt has swung. The birds have seen the boat and they are up with a roar of wings. The gun is no longer bearing, owing to the swing of the punt, but the birds are flying in the same direction as the muzzle is turning. The gunner has one desperate last throw. He whips the gun up to maximum elevation and pulls the lanyard for a flying shot.

A hollow boom fills the estuary. Waders fly screaming and piping down the tide line. A cloud of white smoke drifts away across the water. There is not a single wigeon down on the sands or in the water. The shot was well behind. The birds – there must have been three hundred of them – are settling a mile off on the open sea.

Later on, down towards the river mouth, the punters find fifteen mallard sitting out on open water. There is a fair lop on and the sculler brings them in cleverly within sixty yards. Fifty yards and the birds are still not troubled. Suddenly the gunner kicks the side of the boat. The birds hear the noise and jump. Instantly he pulls the string. There are five mallard dead in the water. They paddle up and collect them. If the gunner hadn't kicked the side of the boat he would probably have got even less. The noise set the birds springing. On the water the wavelets would have shielded them from most of the charge. With their wings open and their bodies slightly raised from the surface they were much more vulnerable.

Eight hours later the punters row back to base. They still have only five duck. More often they have none, so they are not displeased. This is pretty well the way punting turns out.

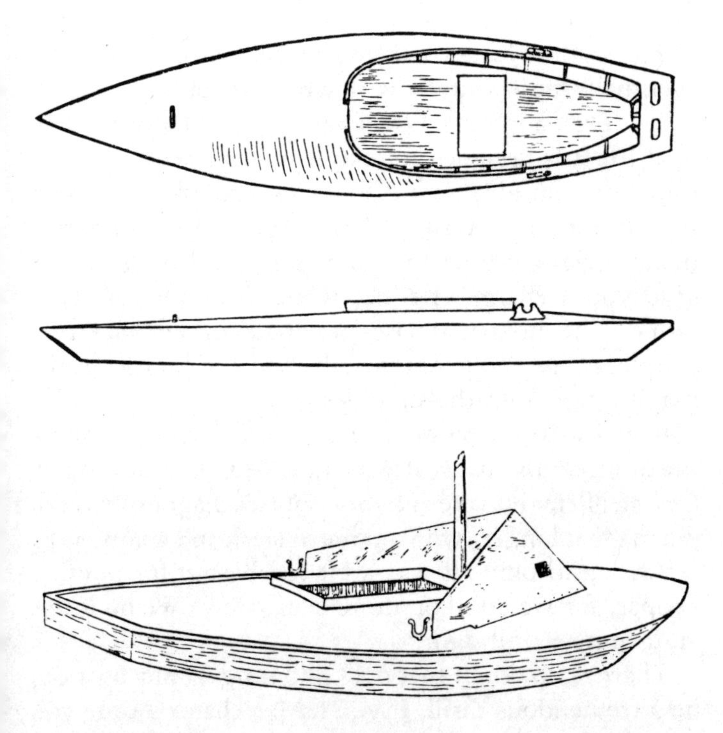

Above, Colonel Peter Hawker's light boat with a maximum beam of 3ft. 4in. This was the basis of the punt designed by Jack Hargreaves and myself and built by Jack. *Below*, an early American sneak-boat for creek creeping. The front apron is removable.

Not all wildfowlers will wish to become punters. But they may at times want to have a shot at it in enclosed waters – or even to creep up creeks with a shoulder gun.

The punt which I and my partner Jack Hargreaves eventually built ourselves (I wrote about it in a book called *The Gun-Punt Adventure*) was essentially a 'sneak boat'. It was designed for single punting with a double four-bore, an ideal small punt-gun provided that both barrels can be fired together. (Again, Bland used to make a double-four for punt gunners). Both barrels give you a charge of 6 oz. which is ample for creek work. The boat was also designed for ferrying two people safely about our marsh, and for forays on the making tide with the shoulder gun.

It was a compromise design and like most compromises it had its snags. It was modelled on a drawing of Colonel Peter Hawker's light-boat (see diagram) though we made it longer, with a pointed stern and slimmer, to act as a gun-punt. It was a bit too beamy for punting proper, for we erred on the side of safety. We built this craft quite a time ago.

There is no doubt that duck shooting from a boat can be a tremendous thrill. If you have a chance I urge you to try it.

WILD FLIGHT

However exciting duck and geese may be when intercepted inland, they only take on their true values when found beyond the sea-wall. There is all the difference between a tame flight and a wild one, even though the first term is a misnomer: there is no such thing as a 'tame' duck when airborne. There is, however, a world dividing mere duck shooting from wildfowling. Wildfowling is a thing of the estuaries and mud flats, and, in this setting, shooting not only becomes inexpressibly more exciting but also much more difficult.

To a large extent the same pattern of behaviour governs the duck. They flight at dawn and dusk. By day they sit out on the sea, and at evening they flight in to feed on the fields or inland flashes, or even on the marsh itself. But there are other and more subtle influences at work, and weather is the most obvious of these. Duck seem to sense a coming storm. Before a big blow they may move in to the saltings in daylight. During a storm they may well stay in the green of the marsh all day, squatting in the bottoms of creeks until put up by a fowler or gunshot and then flighting to another creek nearby. Then the wildfowler can enjoy great sport.

The same may be true during a big freeze-up inland. Duck will fly a hundred or more miles if the ice shuts them out of reservoirs, lakes and ponds, and move down to the salt water which, offshore at least, is bound to be open. But the sport then is likely to be worth while for only a short period. After a week or so of hard frost the fowl will become thin from hunger and trusting with fatigue. It is then a shame, and no sport at all, to shoot them. They should be left to recover as they have troubles enough of their own. This is when WAGBI asks wildfowlers to operate a voluntary ban on shooting until the thaw comes. In hard weather on the East coast I have known ducks fall to shot and instantly become glued to the ice. I have picked them up with their tongues stuck, frozen, to their upper mandibles. There is no sense or humanity in shooting under these conditions. In a freeze-up like this, when there are blocks of pack ice in the creeks, it is not rare to find wading birds frozen to the mud and covered with white coats of frost, like the sentinels at Pompeii who were caught, killed, and enveloped at their posts by volcanic dust.

The situation on the salt marsh is further complicated by the action of the tides. The duck may wish to come in to the marsh to shelter from a storm, but the saltings at that moment may be covered by a high tide. Tide is the second factor that affects their comings and goings, for it covers and uncovers feeding grounds and resting places so that neither tide nor wind can be considered in isolation. Their effect on the movements of fowl is a combined one and it is capable of an enormous number of permutations.

To all this you can add the influence of the moon, for this not only governs the height and extent of tides, but it also, as in inland flighting, dictates when duck will flight at evening and morning.

Add to these things the loneliness of the saltings, the

complete sense of isolation that they give a so-called civilized man, the spice of danger that is always there even for the man who does watch the tide and is completely at home with the geography of every creek and you have some of the fascination of true wildfowling.

The attraction does not, of course, end there. Most salt-marsh wildfowlers are romantics. They breathe the salt air, see the dawn, watch the day die, hear cries and sounds that are a thousand miles from a pay packet or television set. The duck and the geese and the shooting are not everything, not by any means.

Before taking a step over the sea-wall you must think carefully about your clothing. Inland, almost anything warm and loose will do. You can always get back to the car after flight. On the salt marsh you are often out for twelve hours at a stretch; the tides dictate things that way. The first consideration is to stay dry. Once wet, you are miserable. It is fairly easy to stop the rain penetrating, but this, alas, does not always mean that you will remain dry inside your waterproofs. You are faced with a choice between the complete waterproof that shuts out the rain but traps the sweat (because it does not breathe) and the sweater that breathes but lets in the rain.

The easy solution would seem to be to plump for the complete waterproofs. But try slogging out in the dark to a morning flighting position a mile beyond the sea wall over a terrain that seems to be composed of thick black treacle. After two hundred yards you will be in a muck-sweat. After a mile you will be an exhausted grease blob. Worse, when you settle down in a creek, or in the shallow 'grave' you dig yourself in the sand or even mud, you will rapidly cool and feel as though you have been packed in ice.

I admit that everyone has a different thermal system. Friends of mine can make these trips in waterproofs and two sweaters and remain in reasonably good shape. I am the opposite. I very quickly generate heat, even on a very cold day, so long as I am moving. Possibly this has something to do with possessing a very good circulation; indeed, I think serious wildfowling would be very unpleasant, in fact, sheer torture, if you felt the cold too badly. It is useless for me to dress up prior to flighting in my full regalia. Some years ago I found my own personal solution. This was to carry an army surplus back pack – a valise. This is worn over the shoulders, rucksack fashion, and does not hinder shooting nearly so much as a side haversack does, if you suddenly need to take a quick snap at a duck jumping out of a mud gutter.

If it is a dry cold morning I wear one light sweater for the approach march and stick my other sweaters and top waterproof coverings in the pack. Then, when I am in position and glowing with exercise, I put these on to hold the warmth as long as possible. If it is wet, then I strip off all sweaters and carry *them* in the haversack on my back, wearing only the waterproof.

Some other thoughts about clothing. To stay warm, mere thickness of clothing is not so important. What really matters is insulation. Several layers of thin stuff with pockets of air in between them are far better than a solid wedge of heavy sweaters.

Starting from the bottom up then. First, waders (gumboots are useless). Inside the waders a thin pair of ordinary socks with oiled sea-boot stockings over them.

From the waist down. Pyjama trousers. Never forsake pyjama trousers unless you prefer 'long Johns'. They are the key to the lower-level insulation system. Over them, any old trousers you like. They needn't (in fact shouldn't) be too heavy, as, over the top of them, you're going to wear waterproofs. I agree that this bottom rig may generate uncomfortable heat during an approach march but the waterproofs are essential once you get into position. A salt marsh is never dry to sit down in. Nor is it worth carrying the waterproof trousers in your haversack. They are almost impossible to put on over waders.

Colouring of clothing is important. For daylight, drab green or brown, grey even, or a camouflage mixture of all three. In moonlight nothing is better than off-white, the punt-gunner's traditional and necessary uniform. Black shows up abominably on a bright night. On the head you can wear what you like. Some favour a floppy hat with a pull-down brim to hide the face. I rather fancy a woolly cap which keeps the ears warm without covering them. Balaclavas are not so good, just because they do cover the ears. Hearing is a key sense when flighting on the marsh.

What you carry in your back pack after that is up to you. If I'm out on a long trip, I always put in a spare pair of wader socks. Nothing is more miserable than going in over the top of your boots in the first half hour and being stuck with wet socks for the rest of the expedition. If you've got dry thick socks you can achieve some comfort by emptying out your boots, drying the surplus water out of them (by wiping them inside with the wrung-out wet socks) and then putting the boots on again over the dry socks from your pack.

Your haversack can also carry cartridges, hand extractor (important), a small Thermos of warm drink (rather than spirits), string for carrying home a great number of dead duck (rarely needed), field glasses (essential in my view: watching is as good as shooting) and compass in case fog comes down. Incidentally, useful though a compass is, it is far better to know the marsh thoroughly or go with someone who does than to rely on compass bearings. You can march off by compass only to find your way blocked by a deep creek already filled with tide. With or without a compass you need to know the creek system. The last thing that I would seriously recommend carrying is a small Dunlopillo sit-upon cushion. Even in waterproof trousers this can make the difference between a wet bottom and a dry one. Two other thoughts: lighter-fuel handwarmers are excellent and they are cheap, and tube of lip grease saves painful chaps. A wigeon or mallard caller, too, perhaps.

Finally, tide tables. Do not carry these with you, but carry their message in your head. Know when the tide will be high and how high it will be. Then you can judge the moment at which to beat a retreat back to the sea-wall. Always leave early rather than late.

All that I have said assumes that you are making a major excursion. For quick trips out to morning or evening flight you can use any proportion of these etceteras you think fit, though the basic rules remain the same – stay dry and stay warm. That's the only way you'll shoot well and enjoy yourself.

It is quite unpardonable when duck shooting close to water, and particularly on salt marshes, to go out without a dog. Unpicked wounded birds are a calamity for any kind of shooter and inevitably they happen to the wildfowler as much as to the inland rough shooter. When they happen, they must be gathered and knocked on the head as an act of mercy, and as quickly as possible.

Now, an old cock pheasant who decides to hide himself is hard enough to find on dry land. But a duck has another dimension of evasion for, he can dive underwater when in trouble. Even dabbling ducks, when wounded, show an astonishing ability for going down and staying down.

They can swim great distances also. There is nothing more distressing than to watch a 'swimmer' moving fast out of range of the *coup de grace* you owe him. A dog is, of course, the answer, but if for some reason you don't have one with you then you must give the bird a second barrel on the water if you possibly can, before he swims out of shot.

Naturally, the first requirement in a wildfowling dog is a talent for water-work. Most dogs like swimming but some lack the essential flare for retrieving in water, and particularly in rough water. I know one labrador who anticipates the next move of a wounded duck that is trying to dive to avoid him. Somehow he manages to predict its next surfacing point and to be there to intercept it. Another brilliant water dog, a labrador-springer cross in this case, will actually make a shallow dive after the duck and sometimes come up with it.

I myself am a springer man. I once had an immensely strong black and white springer who would swim half a mile on a freezing morning for a bird. I have seen him come ashore with a duck in his mouth and his coat spangled with ice needles. I have to admit, though, that he had his limitations. His colouring was against him for one thing. Though he sat very still at flight times, his coat was not the ideal camouflage for blending with the landscape. Again, when I have sent him to gather a runner at evening flight, incoming duck have spotted his moving, piebald form and sheered off, whereas I am pretty sure they would not have detected a yellow or black labrador. Incidentally, I now have a black labrador.

A spaniel, however tough, is at a disadvantage on the salt marsh, for sticky mud is a necessary ingredient of most saltings. A mud-coated springer, every feather plastered with clinging ooze, is not the happiest of dogs, particularly when he has to sit for several hours in a biting wind. But whether he's happy or not, it is not fair on the dog.

There is another point to consider. Though many spaniels clean themselves like cats within an hour or two of coming in from shooting, their first entrance at the front porch or kitchen door is not likely to be welcome if they have just come fresh – if that is the word – from the nearest mud gutter. I know that gun dogs should be kept outside, but I suspect that a lot of wildfowlers these days go in for dual-purpose dogs who live with the family as well as go shooting. Nowadays you can buy zip-up bags in which to put them – the head naturally remains outside – while they are drying. I often pop my spaniel in a big sack, tying the neck with binder twine!

All this compels me to admit reluctantly that, in my view, labradors are a far better bet than spaniels for the wildfowler pure and simple. Many of us like to combine rough shooting with wildfowling and only have room for one dog, what with children and the other paraphernalia of sheer living. In this case a good strong springer like mine may be a fair compromise solution.

Again, there are many who prefer labradors for rough shooting as well.

There is one other possibility and this is an Irish water spaniel. They are tough, magnificent in water as their name implies, look more like poodles than spaniels and are reputedly remarkably wilful and individualistic. These days they are out of fashion, which seems a pity, for our forefathers swore by them.

Morning flight for duck on the saltings is, in my experience, a chancey business. You are on the receiving end of the flight-line. The duck are on their way out from night feeding-stations inland. The area of saltings over which they must fly is invariably a vast one to cover. If the duck are coming from far inland, then, ten to one, they will have reached a great height by the time they cross the sea-wall. They will carry on like this until well out to sea then drop almost vertically down. This is doubly true in an area where there is a great deal of shooting from, or near, the sea-wall. Duck and geese soon learn that the wall is a danger point.

There is another possible situation at morning flight. The duck *may not have* gone inland to feed. Instead, they have stayed all night in the tidal pools on the marsh. If so, your problem is to get between them and the sea before flight time comes. This is by no means easy, for, except in really rough weather, the figure of a man walking down the saltings in half light is often enough to put every duck into the air.

Rough weather, then, is the main essential for coming to terms with duck at morning flight. Rough weather and an early start. If you plan to get between duck in the top of the marsh and the sea, then your only hope is to creep past them in pitch darkness.

To take the first situation again. Let's say the duck are flighting back from inland fields and pools to the saltings. Early in the year they may be coming from new feeding grounds, such as stubbles, and normal flight lines will therefore probably be altered. Even later in the season flight lines may fluctuate with changes of water level, weather conditions, cleaning up of food supplies at one feeding ground and so on. But there are always likely to be regular flight lines that attract some duck throughout the season, and you can depend on it that these will be well known to, and heavily shot by, the locals. Even though you choose to flight in mid-week when fewer local gunners can be expected, the effect of their week-end shooting will in all probability keep the duck comfortably out of gunshot. The answer again is rough weather.

The key to all these changing positions of flight line is local knowledge, best of all acquired by your own observation (which more or less means you must live on the spot), but bought, if all else fails, from a local guide. If you employ one of these make sure he *is* a wildfowler. Sometimes he's more interested in the pheasants that hop over the top of the sea bank from inland shoots.

Even in a strange place, however, you can deduce some things about probable flight lines from use of the map and your own knowledge of duck. Look for inland lakes, and especially old decoy ponds – they weren't put there for nothing. Look for marsh land running down to the sea from high ground, for river valleys, and even for quite small streams. Duck will follow water in preference to anything else, though sometimes natural contours like a steep valley will attract them if the sea is at one end and a sheet of inland water at the other.

If you find a large pile of cartridge cases along a certain thirty yard stretch of the sea-wall do not assume that this is a regular crossing point. Fowlers have been known to scatter their empties in the wrong places to confuse the issue as far as visitors are concerned. If the cartridges are all of the same make and shot size, then you may have cause to be doubly suspicious. If the cases come from different gunmakers and the shot sizes or bores vary, then this may be a flighting point used regularly by a number of guns. You need to know almost as much about the habits of wildfowlers as you do about the fowl themselves.

However, I have had some magnificent morning flights on the sea-wall before now. One I remember particularly in Anglesey was within a hundred yards of the pub in which the local wildfowling club had its headquarters. There was a gale blowing that morning and the duck came beating down the river valley to drop just behind the wall into the harbour. Note, though, that everything was just right. The wind was in their faces and the tide was at full flood. They didn't want to fly any further and the water was there for them to drop on.

Now for situation two. Finding the duck in the top of the marsh also depends on weather and tide conditions. Ideally, you want a period just after a spring tide when fresh pools have been formed in the green of the marsh, pools that are surrounded by salt marsh plants like samphire. Teal have a great love of samphire seeds. If you blunder into one of these flashes on a dark morning you may put the duck up at your feet, but a single bird, or at best two, is all you are likely to get. You must get to seaward of your birds well before light and then hide in a creek. Creeks are not only important for providing cover. The main ones are frequently used as high roads by travelling duck and waders and, though the majority of birds that come your way from the marsh-top pools as it gets light are likely to be wigeon, there's no telling what may turn up – a bunch of pintail, mallard, or a veering, hurtling party of teal, not to mention curlew and redshank if you have a mind to shoot waders.

On these mornings the secret is to get up and get out early enough. If you are not well in position before the first dawn streaks appear, then you might just as well have stayed in bed. Local knowledge of the saltings is vital to success here. You may have allowed enough time to reach your position but find when half way there that the tide has not ebbed sufficiently to allow you to cross a main creek. So you wait impotently while dawn comes up and the tide drops, by which time the duck have all passed wide of you.

The lesson of the filled creek is that close study of the Tide Tables allied with local knowledge is not only vital to success as well as safety but half the fun of the business. With coastal wildfowling, the planning of the campaign is often as much sport as the shooting. I don't have to emphasize that though an unexpectedly ebbing tide may be irritating, it is not dangerous. A flowing tide coupled with lack of know-how can prove fatal: it all too frequently has done so. It is very easy to get cut off on a strange marsh. Always plan your line of retreat and plan it in time. If there are islands then note which ones remain high and dry at full flood. If you have left it too late to get back to the sea-wall as the tide makes, then, at the very worst, you can sit out the tide on a hunk of dry land and may, incidentally, get some shooting from it.

If a big tide coincides with storm conditions extreme caution is necessary, especially on the east coast in the Thames, Medway and East Anglian river estuaries. Get a meteorological report for the area.

But back to morning flight. Though rough weather is always the thing to hope for, it's only fair to say I have enjoyed some exciting, not to say utterly beautiful, flights on fine, still, clear mornings. Unknown to you, there may be some factor that is keeping the duck in the marsh and is persuading them to move around between creeks. Usually this situation won't last for more than three or four shots. After that, the duck will become alarmed and take off *en masse* for sea. But I have bagged four or five birds before now on some memorably fine mornings.

Sometimes it is worth staying out on the marsh after morning flight is over, but not often. There are two things that can make it profitable: the first is tide, and the second, as always, weather.

When the wind is howling in off the sea, preferably with a bit of snow in it, the duck will be very reluctant to face dawn take-off. Even if some flight, they are liable to come drifting back into the marsh for shelter as the morning wears on. To take full advantage of this you want a marsh from which the tide has retreated, giving the duck maximum choice of resting creeks. In this situation it is very useful to have an experienced companion or two with you so that you can keep the birds moving about. If the tide is full on these mornings you are likely to draw a blank. The duck may pack in to sit on sheltered water but they will be perpetually out of range. Your best chance then is to follow the ebb out. If it's still blowing hard enough the duck won't want to leave. They'll simply settle down into the creeks and may even begin to feed. Though you'll put some of them up when making your way down the marsh behind the tide, some should remain – provided the wind is strong enough and from the right direction. A wind blowing seawards is useless. It will take the duck with it.

Sometimes, quite divorced from really rough weather, there is a tidal flight. Duck that have been resting on exposed muds will become flooded off, particularly by a spring tide. If the wind is out to sea they'll probably fly towards open water. But with a bit of a breeze off the sea they may move in with the tide, a bit at a time. For this kind of shooting you need a marsh with high land in the shape of islands or causeways, otherwise you will be constantly falling back ahead of the birds. You will also need a dog or boat for retrieving. Without some means of recovery, the birds will be infuriatingly swept out of reach by the tide, and, as I have already said, I see no excuse for shooting duck you can't gather. You would be better off shooting clay pigeons.

On such daylight shoots on the marsh, decoys can be useful. There are several important points to consider when choosing decoys. Firstly, weighted decoys ride better. The only problem is to carry them out over the saltings. If you've got a boat, then weight doesn't matter. There are now some beautifully made plastic models, one and a half times life-size, with accurate matt finishes and weighted keels. The best used to be Italian but now there are some excellent British ones.

I do not think that colouring matters a bit. Beautifully painted wooden deeks are pure joy to behold. Personally, I use them in all their glory as doorsteps at home.

If colour has little importance, attitude certainly has. A duck with its head up is often an alarmed, or at least an alert, duck. When I buy wooden decoys I go for some dozers, those with their heads well tucked into their breast feathers. These are contented duck without a hint of danger and the kind of duck other duck like to see. I notice that the Americans, who are great decoy makers, often shoot over birds with their heads tucked back to front in the true duck attitude of repose. These, I feel, are the most satisfactory decoys of all.

As with all deeks, the great thing is to create a pattern of natural calm. Duck on dry land will prefer to sit head to wind, but they won't all do so dressed by the right like a Guards platoon. Some will be slightly across wind. Duck on water will normally breast the current, though here you have no problems; all you need to do is attach the mooring string to an eye at the front of the bird, provided the tide is making, and at the rear end if it is ebbing. Normally, decoys will be used on a making tide or at low water.

Light rubber deeks are made for easy carrying. There are solid rubber models which are quite compact. You can easily squash ten into an old army pack, provided there is nothing else in it.

Fold-up decoys are sometimes used. These are made of very thin rubber or plastic and can be screwed up to the size of a cigarette packet. The trick is that their base contains a heavy metal ring. When the decoys are lobbed out on to the water, they unwrap parachute-fashion as they fly and then hit the water metal-ring first. This blow drives sufficient air into the body to inflate it and make the decoys sit naturally. A marble, pocketed in a fold of rubber at the front, makes a fixture for the mooring string. Good as these decoys are, in rough weather I have seen them fill and eventually half sink.

Silhouette decoys can work quite well when laid out on the mud. The snag here is that enough will have to be laid cross-wind to catch the incoming duck's attention. Some must also be set at right angles to the main batch so that when the duck swing round to settle they will not lose sight of the decoys altogether.

The best decoy flight I remember was in a shallow mud-lagoon close to the sea-wall on the Wash. The tide was making, there was snow blowing in the gale that roared in from the sea. We put our solid rubber decoys out on the mud just after light and shot, on and off, all morning at parties of duck, and even a few geese, that came into the decoys imagining that some of their friends had found shelter. On this occasion one member of the party had a wigeon-caller that definitely swung several teetering bunches of duck in the air. Wigeon whistles often work on their own. Coupled with decoys (which were mallard-pattern, incidentally) they are doubly effective. It is also possible to call teal in by imitating their discordant double whistle. Mallard will often swing to this, too. Pintail can be called with a mechanical mallard caller. The best kind are the corrugated rubber hose type, you waggle to produce the noise.

Here is another strange fact: the species represented by decoys does not seem to matter. Mallard-shaped deeks will attract anything, at least among the dabbling duck. It is the duck shape that counts, which brings us back to the unimportance of colour.

There is only one possible exception to this rule, and that is the use of a white bird as attractor and focal point. I have often noticed how mallard and wigeon will swing in to real shelduck sitting out on water. Shellies appear black and white at a distance, and, of course, it is the white that shows. I believe there may be a case for making a shelduck decoy (or maybe even a small gull). Though shelduck are protected there is no reason why you shouldn't enlist their aid to lure other species.

Now for afternoon on the marsh. Except in rough-weather conditions this is usually a blank period. It can sometimes produce a bag before the onset of a storm. Duck do seem to have foreknowledge of bad weather on the way. I recall going out on a Norfolk marsh in full daylight at three in the afternoon. The tide was low, though beginning to make. The day was abominably fine. Just the same, we walked into three or four hundred teal preening and apparently feeding in tidal pools. Even the first four birds shot did not seem entirely to persuade the others to leave. Parties of seven and eight kept swinging back until flight time. When it began to get dusk the whole gang, plus quite a few wigeon, started piling back in earnest. We had some exciting shooting and for no apparent reason that one could see. By nine o'clock that evening the wind had shifted round and was blowing half a gale that built up to a full gale by morning. I can only think those duck knew, perhaps through the change in atmospheric pressure, or by some sense that humans do not have, that a big blow was on the way. The hard weather that storm brought lasted for a week. Possibly it is altogether too fanciful to suggest that those teal had made up their minds to get their feed while the going was good. Snow fell and lay on the marsh and surrounding district for a week following the onset of the gale, and many inland waters were frozen up.

The true wildfowler's duck is, of course, the wigeon, and it is this bird that gives the best of evening flights on the saltings. Wigeon are extremely fussy about their food. As long as the grasses are to their liking, they will stay and make the most of things. The moment the food falls below the standard they demand, they are off to some other feeding ground. Wigeon were once essentially sea and salt marsh birds. Now with the disappearance of *Zostera marina* they increasingly feed inland. Nevertheless, I believe that they prefer to stay and feed on the saltings when conditions are attractive to them. So I always think of wigeon when going to evening flight beyond the sea-wall.

Evening can be as tricky as morning flighting. The constants of coastal flighting – weather and tide – as usual govern everything. But in the evening you can add another key ingredient – the amount of moonlight.

About the worst combination of events I can think of is a blank moon, an evening without a breath of wind, and a dead low tide. With this set-up the duck will probably sit dozing happily on the calm waters, far out, until the last possible moment. The marsh will be dry and unattractive to them. So they will take off late and flicker over as small as starlings, bound for inland destinations. Your only hope then is to get as far down the marsh and as close to take-off point as possible. Usually you will fail to score. The situation has its compensations though. You will see some magnificent sunsets while living in a world which few townspeople can even imagine. It is like standing on the moon, and when the cottage lights start to go on inland you feel as cut off from them as a space traveller looking back at earth. The lights have their attraction at a distance as an emphasis to loneliness. When you eventually come off, cold and hungry, they have their attraction at close quarters also. These pleasures are very real by-products of wildfowling.

The best of wigeon flighting on the marsh is done in the full, or nearly full, moon. Then you can sometimes find birds working along the tide edge all night long. A full moon on its own is almost useless. To begin with, you will not see the birds against a clear sky until it is far too late; it is also practically impossible to judge their speed and direction. Equally disastrous is the fact that the wigeon will see you. Face and hands stand out like lamps in full, clear moonlight. Shadows are as tell-tale as floodlit figures. Black waders show up as if coated with Day-Glo paint. If there is any colour that can help hide you in this light, then I think it is a dirty off-white, much as you would use in snow.

What you really need is a big moon covered with a layer of high cloud. This gives you a perfect shooting light, and silhouettes the birds against the sky.

Provided there is cover, or the moon is sufficiently hidden, you can get shooting all night long on a making tide, simply by falling back ahead of it. Better still, find some water high up on the marsh which the wigeon want. An ideal situation is made just after the highest spring tides when the sea has been right up to the wall and filled pools which are normally not duck haunts. The water will only stay in these for a limited time, but you have only to spot wigeon feathers and droppings round these in daylight to know that the night will produce a good moonlight flight.

One of the best wigeon flights I have heard of in these conditions was made by the late Kenzie Thorpe, the great Wash professional, on a snowy moonlight night during the war. He knew the duck were using this tidal lagoon. He had a flowing tide, a snow storm, moon and cloud in his favour. He had a rare thing in those days, an unopened box of 100 cartridges. He had shot out by midnight and gathered sixty-three wigeon.

That's the sort of shooting the marsh can provide, though, to be frank, it seldom does. Bags of half-a-dozen duck are something with which to be pleased. But the fascination of the saltings is not in the bag alone. A wild flight is the cream of duck shooting.

APPENDIX I

COOKING WILD DUCK

The great difference between wild and tame duck is that there is virtually no fat on the former. They will therefore quickly become dry if overdone. There is an old saying that wild duck should merely be allowed to fly through a very hot oven. This is going too far. All the same they should be very lightly done and must be kept moist by basting, by laying slices of fat bacon over the breasts, or by wrapping in tin foil which is opened to brown the breasts at the last stage of cooking. They are essentially birds that need under- rather than overdoing. I believe they should be started on a low gas and then the oven made very hot during the last half hour. We roast ours for at least one hour.

Duck do become more tender if hung for a week or so, but the weather needs to be cold. I normally hang mine with the guts in; if the weather is mild it will pay to clean them. I would never hang duck in mild conditions more than two or three days.

Mallard and teal present few difficulties in preparation, except perhaps in the plucking, for the feathers are firmly fixed. Don't bother with the wings. There is little flesh on them and they are best cut off at the roots after plucking. If you remove them first, you may cut your fingers on sharp bones.

Wigeon may taste 'fishy' late in the season. Shoveler often taste muddy. These birds are improved by being placed in a solution of vinegar and water, or even salt and water, overnight. Cooking with an onion or two inside also helps. Early season wigeon are usually sweet enough for straight roasting. Later on it may pay to casserole them with mushrooms and so on. Wigeon off fresh marshes and grass feeding compare with any duck for sweetness and succulence.

The etceteras are important with wild duck. Orange salad made with sections of fresh orange garnished with French dressing goes well with any kind of wild duck. Apple sauce is delicious with mallard. Any form of onion and sage stuffing packed inside duck or wigeon is acceptable, though teal, I feel, are so delightful that they need no more than the addition of a slice or two of crisp fat bacon preferably cooked with the bird.

If you want a special sauce then I recommend the following:

1 saltspoon salt,
½ saltspoon cayenne pepper,
1 dessertspoonful lemon juice,
1 dessertspoonful lemon juice,
1 dessertspoonful sugar,
2 dessertspoonfuls Harvey's sauce,
3 dessertspoonfuls port wine.
Mix and heat. Pour over the bird, having first sliced it lightly so that the juices may mix with the sauce. Serve in the sauce resulting from the mixture.

The best variation on the straight roasting procedure with wild duck is the one my wife has adapted from a recipe for the farmyard variety. It is magnificent.

You need: 1 mallard, 1 glass red wine, 2 heads celery,

1 large onion thinly sliced, 2 tablespoons salted cashew nuts, 1 oz. butter. Then for the sauce: 3 tablespoons oil, 3 tablespoons diced onions, carrots and celery, 2 level tablespoons flour, 1 teaspoon tomato purée, one glass red wine, 1½ pints stock.

Heat the oil, put in the vegetables and allow barely to colour. Stir in the flour and cook to a rich brown. Add the purée, wine and two thirds of the stock. Bring to boil and simmer for 35 minutes. Add the rest of the stock in two parts, bringing the sauce to the boil and skimming between each addition. When syrupy, spread the duck with butter and roast with the wine in a hot oven for 45–50 minutes. Cut the celery in small pieces, melt the butter in a shallow pan and add onion and celery. Cook for 5 minutes. Arrange this in the bottom of a casserole, carve the flesh off the duck and place it on top. Add nuts, and spoon the sauce over the duck. Cover the dish and set in a slow oven for 15–20 minutes. My wife adds that she is indebted to the Constance E. Spry School of Cookery for this inspiration in the first instance.

Another tip for varying the straight roasting routine: baste your duck with honey before popping it into the oven.

My wife bastes duck with a splendid mixture of brown sugar, mustard and orange juice. The glaze is mixed to taste and must be thick enough to stay put when basted over the duck in the last stage of roasting. The orange peel is placed inside the duck. The baste gives them a delicious crisp glaze.

There is only one further refinement of wild duck cooking I can think of, but for this you need a duck press. *Canard pressé* extracts the very last ounce of duckness out of a duck and is a speciality of some of the best restaurants in the world, including the Tour D'Argent in Paris. But first catch your duck press. They can be bought new but are rare and costly. I'm told that the best way to find one is at a sale of second-hand restaurant equipment.

APPENDIX II

NOTES ON FLIGHTING

Month	*Places to watch*	*Approximate times morning and evening flights** (first of month)
September	Stubbles, flight ponds, inland flight lines	Evenings, 2000 Mornings, 0430
October	Flight ponds, saltings fresh marshes	Evenings, 1900 Mornings, 0550
November	Saltings now coming to best form, also large inland marshes and lakes	Evenings, 1630–1700 Mornings, 0545–0630
December	Fed flight ponds now at premium, saltings good	Evenings, 1600 Mornings, 0630
January	Fed flight ponds now at premium, saltings good	Evenings, 1615 Mornings, 0630
February	Salt marshes only	Evenings, 1715 Mornings, 0600

* These times indicate the approximate earliest time the flight should start in normal conditions.

POSSIBILITIES

Species	*Best opportunities*	*Remarks*
Mallard, teal	E. flight, full moon	Ducks fat and not very wary. Many young birds, also drakes in eclipse
Wigeon arrive end of month	Some gales likely mid-month	Early wigeon tired and thin on arrival. Mallard and teal more careful now
All species coming to winter strength	November full moon best for wigeon, given cloud	Note that clocks altered early Nov., make MF and EF an hour earlier
All species to winter strength	Flight times now becoming conveniently late	Local migrations due to cold spells likely
Mallard and teal often move south	Watch for mid-month gales	Icing conditions may affect movements. Thaw following freeze-ups may produce too much water
All species likely on saltings if cold spell	M.F. getting very early towards end of season	All shooting ends on 20th

APPENDIX III

W.A.G.B.I.

The Wildfowlers' Association of Great Britain and Ireland is the key organization when it comes to safeguarding the sport of duck and goose shooters. Its strength is that it is as interested in conservation as in shooting. It, and its member clubs, work closely with the Nature Conservancy, the Wildfowl Trust and with the Royal Society for the Protection of Birds, as well as sporting organizations such as the British Field Sports Society and the Game Conservancy, and the British Shooting Sports Council.

There is no doubt that there are still people who would like to stop wildfowling, and indeed all shooting. Equally there are stupid people on the shooting side. There is too much irresponsible shooting round the coasts these days by gunners who come out from inland districts without knowing or caring about wildfowl.

WAGBI's aim is to check these people where they do harm and convert them into proper wildfowlers if there is half a chance.

Solidarity is vital in the sport and WAGBI is every shore gunner's best chance of obtaining it. I therefore strongly urge all wildfowlers to join WAGBI. The address is: Marford Mill, Rossett, Clwyd LL12 0HL, North Wales.